SAT

Vocabulary-Building Flashcards

Vocabulary Building Games

PLUS Word Builder Chart
For Windows®

Premium Edition with CD-ROM

Staff of Research & Education Association

Research & Education Association
Visit our website at
www.rea.com

Research & Education Association
61 Ethel Road West
Piscataway, New Jersey 08854
E-mail: info@rea.com

**Vocabulary-Building Flashcard Book
for the SAT
Premium Edition with CD-ROM**

Printed in the United States of America

Library of Congress Control Number 2008932468

ISBN-13: 978-0-7386-0472-5
ISBN-10: 0-7386-0472-0

H08-0101

About This Premium Edition with CD-ROM

SAT test experts all agree that building a powerful SAT-specific vocabulary is the single most important way you can raise your score on the Critical Reading and Writing sections of the test.

This **Premium CD Edition** of REA's best-selling book contains 900 flashcards with the most frequently used words on the SAT, as well as **Verbal Building Software** and a **Vocabulary Enhancer Chart on CD.** The software presents games and exercises designed to challenge your flashcard study and improve your SAT reading and vocabulary skills.

Learning and remembering 900 words is not an easy task, especially if many of these words are new to you. This unique flashcard book is designed to help you in your quest. Each page presents the flashcard word with space to write in your definition of the word. On the flip side of each page you'll find the correct definition of the word, its part of speech (adjective, verb, etc.), and sample sentences using the word in context.

It's a three-step learning process:

1. See the word.

2. Write in your definition.

3. Flip the page over and compare your definition to the correct one.

You will also find that flashcards in a book have several advantages over flashcards in a box. You don't have to cope with hundreds of loose cards. Whenever you want to study, you can just open the book and get going.

Take this book along with you everywhere since there are a lot of words to study and the book is ready to use whenever you are.

Best to start now — test day is drawing near!

08/24/2013   200 પુરા કર્યા છે. done

Questions

08/ 17/

Q1

PALINDROME

*Your Own Answer*_____

_____

Q2

ADAGE

*Your Own Answer*_____

_____

Q3

HACKNEYED

*Your Own Answer*_____

_____

Correct Answers

A1

n.—a word or phrase which reads the same backward and forward

"Bob," "Dad," and "Madam" are examples of **palindromes**.

A2

n.—an old saying now accepted as being truthful

"Do unto others as you wish them to do unto you" is still one of the most widely quoted **adages**.

A3

adj.—made common by overuse

"Have a nice day" has become something of a **hackneyed** expression.

Questions

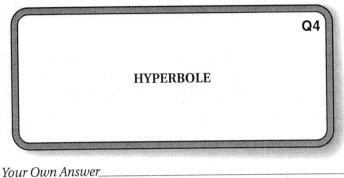

Q4

HYPERBOLE

*Your Own Answer*_____

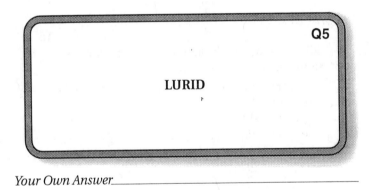

Q5

LURID

*Your Own Answer*_____

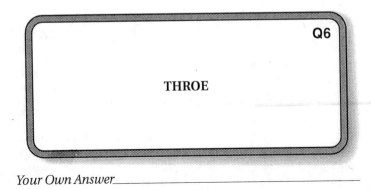

Q6

THROE

*Your Own Answer*_____

Correct Answers

n.—an exaggeration, not to be taken seriously

"The full moon was almost blinding in its brightness," he said with a measure of **hyperbole**.

adj.—1. glowing through haze; 2. shocking; sensational

1. A **lurid** sun shone upon them as they watched it set on the beach.
2. The tabloid specialized in **lurid** stories about celebrities' indiscretions.

n.—spasm or pang

A particularly violent **throe** in her left knee knocked her off her feet.

Questions

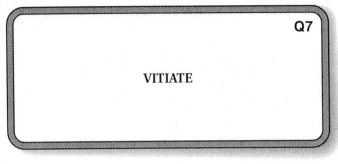

Q7

VITIATE

*Your Own Answer*_____

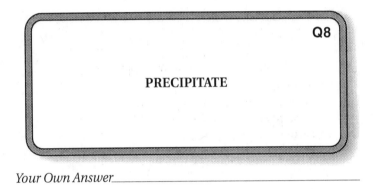

Q8

PRECIPITATE

*Your Own Answer*_____

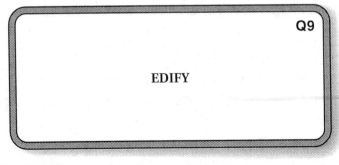

Q9

EDIFY

*Your Own Answer*_____

Correct Answers

A7

v.—1. to spoil; 2. to cause moral weakness

1. A rainstorm will **vitiate** our plans for a day of hiking.
2. Watching adult movies may **vitiate** the minds of young children.

A8

1.v.; 2. adj.—1. to cause to happen; 2. happening quickly

1. A rude comment may **precipitate** an argument.
2. The **precipitating** flood caught the village off-guard.

A9

v.—to instruct and improve the mind

The teachers worked to **edify** their students through lessons and discussion.

Questions

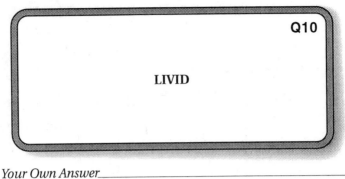

Q10

LIVID

*Your Own Answer*_____

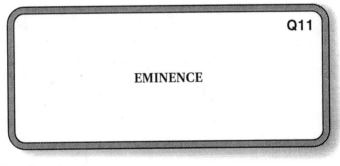

Q11

EMINENCE

*Your Own Answer*_____

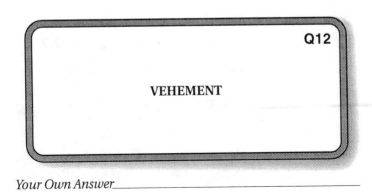

Q12

VEHEMENT

*Your Own Answer*_____

Correct Answers

A10

adj.—1. discolored, as if bruised; 2. extremely angry; furious

1. After the fall, her arm was **livid**.
2. She became **livid** when she heard the news.

A11

n.—1. a lofty place; 2. superiority

1. After toiling in the shadows for years, at last she achieved **eminence**.
2. The **eminence** of the institution can be seen in the impact of its research.

A12

adj.—1. using great force; 2. described by strong feelings

1. After trying for hours, his **vehement** efforts finally yielded some positive results.
2. The artillery hit the enemy's trenches **vehemently**.

Questions

Q13

AMORPHOUS

*Your Own Answer*_____

Q14

CONSORT

*Your Own Answer*_____

Q15

IMMACULATE

*Your Own Answer*_____

Correct Answers

A13

adj.—1. with no shape; 2. unorganized

1. An **amorphous** gel seeped through the cracks.
2. The **amorphous** hiking group lost its way in the forest.

A14

1. n.; 2. v.—1. a companion; a spouse; 2. to associate

1. An elderly woman was seeking a **consort**.
2. They waited until dark to **consort** under the moonlight.

A15

adj.—perfectly clean; correct
An **immaculate** house is free of dust or clutter.

Questions

Q16

UNTOWARD

*Your Own Answer*_____

_____

Q17

ASTRINGENT

*Your Own Answer*_____

_____

Q18

CHARY

*Your Own Answer*_____

_____

Correct Answers

A16

adj.—unfortunate

All of their friends expressed sympathy about their **untoward** separation.

A17

1. n.; 2. adj.—1. a substance that contracts bodily tissues; 2. harsh; biting

1. **Astringent** is used to help tighten pores of the skin.

2. Her **astringent** remarks at the podium would not soon be forgotten.

A18

adj.—cautious

Children must be **chary** when they go trick or treating on Halloween.

Questions

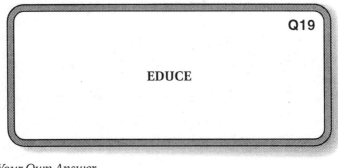

Q19

EDUCE

*Your Own Answer*_____

_____

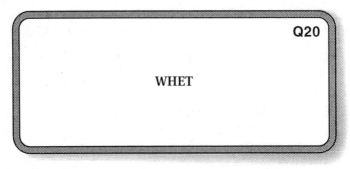

Q20

WHET

*Your Own Answer*_____

_____

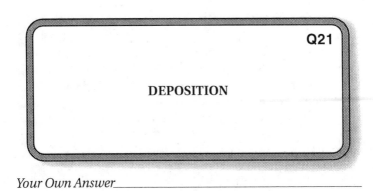

Q21

DEPOSITION

*Your Own Answer*_____

_____

Correct Answers

v.—1. to draw out; 2. to infer from information

1. Because she is so quiet, I was forced to **educe** a response.

2. I **educe** from the report that the experiment was a success.

v.—1. to sharpen by rubbing; 2. to stimulate

1. Before carving the turkey, you must **whet** the blade.

2. The smell of cooking food **whetted** my appetite.

n.—1. a removal from office or power; 2. a testimony

1. Failing to act lawfully could result in his **deposition**.

2. She met with her lawyer this morning to review her **deposition**.

Questions

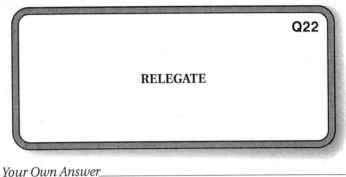

Q22

RELEGATE

*Your Own Answer*_____

Q23

LUCID

*Your Own Answer*_____

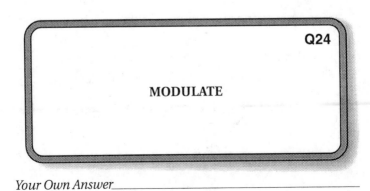

Q24

MODULATE

*Your Own Answer*_____

Correct Answers

v.—1. to assign to an inferior position; 2. to commit to an action

1. The lazy business executive was **relegated** to the mailroom.
2. The president has **relegated** the troops to the mission.

adj.—1. shiny; 2. clear-minded

1. He chose a shimmering, **lucid** fabric for his curtains.
2. When **lucid**, the elderly man spoke of vivid memories.

v.—1. to regulate or adjust; 2. to vary the pitch

1. He **modulated** the color knob on the television set until the picture was perfect.
2. A trained singer knows how to **modulate** her voice to the desired pitch.

Questions

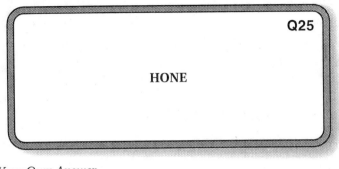

Q25

HONE

*Your Own Answer*_____

_____

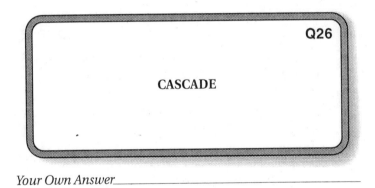

Q26

CASCADE

*Your Own Answer*_____

_____

Q27

COY

*Your Own Answer*_____

_____

Correct Answers

1. n; 2. v.—1. something used to sharpen; 2. to sharpen

1. He ran the knife over the **hone** to get a razor-sharp edge.
2. The apprenticeship will give her the opportunity to **hone** her skills.

n.—1. a small series of waterfalls; 2. something falling in a descending arrangement similar to a waterfall

1. He took a photograph of the lovely **cascade**.
2. The drapes formed a **cascade** down the window.

adj.—1. modest; bashful; 2. pretending shyness to attract

1. Her **coy** manner attracted the man.
2. He's not really that shy; he's just being **coy**.

Questions

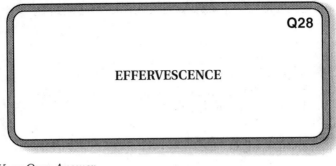

Q28

EFFERVESCENCE

*Your Own Answer*_____

_____

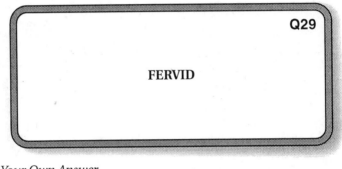

Q29

FERVID

*Your Own Answer*_____

_____

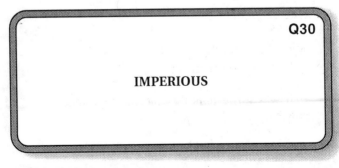

Q30

IMPERIOUS

*Your Own Answer*_____

_____

Correct Answers

A28

n.—1. liveliness; spirit; enthusiasm; 2. bubbliness

1. Her **effervescence** was contagious; she made everyone around her happy.

2. The **effervescence** of champagne is what makes it different from wine.

A29

adj.—1. intensely hot; 2. fervent; impassioned

1. Her **fervid** skin alerted the doctor to her fever.

2. The **fervid** sermon of the preacher swayed his congregation.

A30

adj.—1. arrogant; 2. urgent

1. Her **imperious** manner cost her her two best friends.

2. It was **imperious** that the message reach the police chief.

Questions

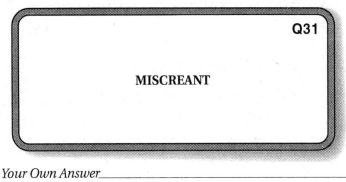

Q31

MISCREANT

*Your Own Answer*_____

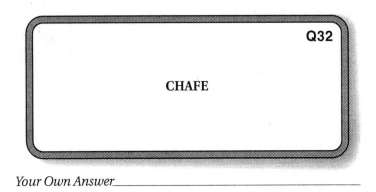

Q32

CHAFE

*Your Own Answer*_____

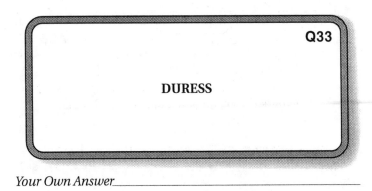

Q33

DURESS

*Your Own Answer*_____

Correct Answers

A31

1. adj.; 2. n.—1. evil; 2. an evil person; villain

1. Her **miscreant** actions shocked and surprised her family.
2. The **miscreant** thought nothing of taking others' money and belongings.

A32

v.—1. to annoy; to irritate; 2. to wear away or make sore by rubbing

1. His constant teasing **chafed** her.
2. He doesn't wear pure wool sweaters because they usually **chafe** his skin.

A33

n.—1. imprisonment; 2. the use of threats

1. His **duress** was supposed to last 10–15 years.
2. The policewoman put the man under **duress** in order to get a confession.

Questions

GOAD

*Your Own Answer*_____

IDEOLOGY

*Your Own Answer*_____

SALIENT

*Your Own Answer*_____

Correct Answers

A34

1. n; 2. v.—1. a driving impulse; 2. to push into action

1. His **goad** urged him to pursue the object of his affection.

2. Thinking about money will **goad** him into getting a job.

A35

n.—1. speculation; 2. representative way of thinking

1. His **ideology** proved to be faulty.

2. The **ideology** of business can be found in the new book.

A36

adj.—1. projecting; 2. noticeable

1. His most **salient** feature is his nose.

2. His **salient** bruise will alert his mother to the altercation.

Questions

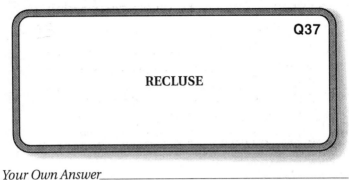

Q37

RECLUSE

*Your Own Answer*_____

_____

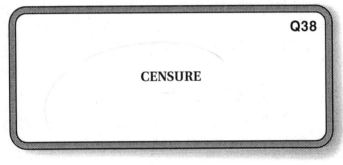

Q38

CENSURE

*Your Own Answer*_____

_____

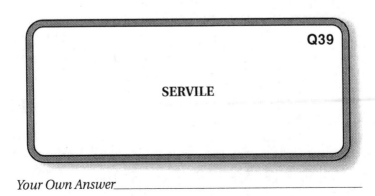

Q39

SERVILE

*Your Own Answer*_____

_____

Correct Answers

A37

1. adj.; 2. n.—1. solitary; 2. a person who lives in seclusion

1. The prisoner lived a **reclusive** life in his tiny cell.

2. The writer lived alone in the country as a **recluse**, free from the distractions of the city.

A38

n.—a strong expression of disapproval

The **censure** given by the critic prevented the movie from winning an Oscar.

A39

adj.—a slave-like manner

The **servile** nurse did everything the doctor told her to do.

Questions

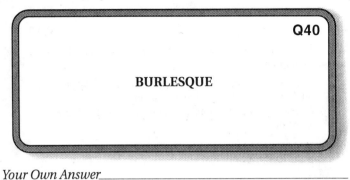

Q40

BURLESQUE

*Your Own Answer*_____

_____

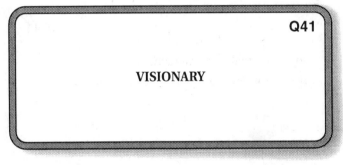

Q41

VISIONARY

*Your Own Answer*_____

_____

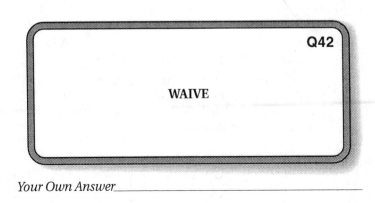

Q42

WAIVE

*Your Own Answer*_____

_____

t Answers

A40

2. n.—1. to imitate in a non-serious manner; 2. a comi-
cal imitation

1. His stump speeches were so hackneyed, he seemed to be
burlesquing his role as a congressman.
2. George Burns was considered one of the great practition-
ers of **burlesque**.

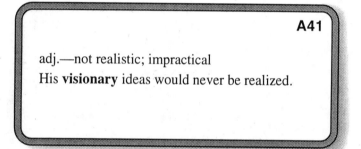

A41

adj.—not realistic; impractical
His **visionary** ideas would never be realized.

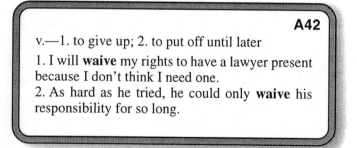

A42

v.—1. to give up; 2. to put off until later
1. I will **waive** my rights to have a lawyer present
because I don't think I need one.
2. As hard as he tried, he could only **waive** his
responsibility for so long.

Questions

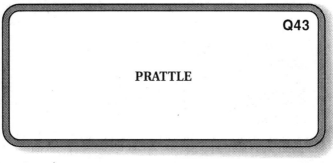

Q43

PRATTLE

*Your Own Answer*_____

Q44

AUSPICIOUS

*Your Own Answer*_____

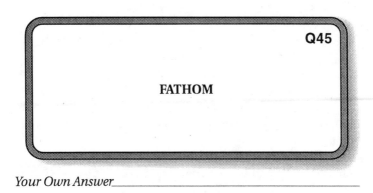

Q45

FATHOM

*Your Own Answer*_____

Correct Answers

1. n.; 2. v.—1. childish babble; 2. to babble while speaking

1. I've listened to his **prattle** for far too long.
2. The toddler does more **prattling** than talking.

adj.—1. of good omen; 2. successful

1. After an **auspicious** start, the football team could not sustain its lead and lost in overtime.
2. The campaign had an **auspicious** start, foreshadowing the candidate's win.

1. v.; 2. n.—1. to understand; 2. a nautical unit of depth equal to 6 feet

1. It was difficult to **fathom** the reason for closing the institution.
2. The submarine cruised at 17 **fathoms** below the surface.

Questions

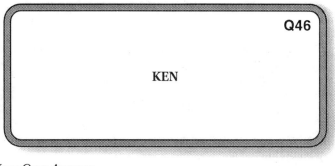

Q46

KEN

*Your Own Answer*_____

_____

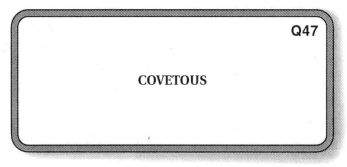

Q47

COVETOUS

*Your Own Answer*_____

_____

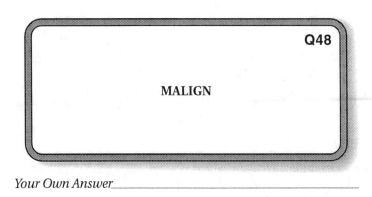

Q48

MALIGN

*Your Own Answer*_____

_____

Correct Answers

A46

1. v.; 2. n.—1. to know; 2. one's understanding

1. It was difficult to **ken** exactly what she had in mind.

2. My **ken** of the situation proved to be incorrect.

A47

adj.—1. greedy; 2. eagerly desirous

1. The child was very **covetous** of his toys and would never share them.

2. Lonnie, **covetous** of education, went to almost every lecture at the university.

A48

1. adj.; 2. v.—1. having an evil disposition toward others (opposite: benign); 2. to speak evil of

1. Many children were afraid to go near the home of the **malign** man.

2. It is easy to **malign** someone you dislike.

Questions

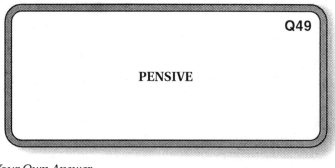

Q49

PENSIVE

*Your Own Answer*_____

Q50

TETHER

*Your Own Answer*_____

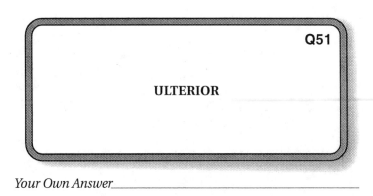

Q51

ULTERIOR

*Your Own Answer*_____

Correct Answers

adj.—1. engaged in deep thought; 2. expressing thoughtfulness with some sadness

1. My hours alone are often more **pensive** than the time I spend with friends.
2. The **pensive** mood was broken by a witty joke.

n.—1. the range or limit of one's abilities; 2. rope or chain used to keep a boat from drifting or an animal from wandering

1. My **tether** of playing basketball is shooting air balls.
2. The bulldog was **tethered** to his doghouse.

adj.—1. regarding the future; 2. undisclosed

1. My **ulterior** concerns are more important than my immediate ones.
2. The man's **ulterior** motive was to spy on the lab, though he said he wanted a job.

Questions

Q52

WANTON

✓

*Your Own Answer*_____

Q53

ODIUM

*Your Own Answer*_____

Q54

SUPERFLUOUS

*Your Own Answer*_____

Correct Answers

A52

adj.—1. unmanageable; 2. unjustifiably malicious

1. My **wanton** hunger must be satiated.
2. With **wanton** aggression, the army attacked the defenseless village.

A53

n.—1. hatred; 2. the disgrace from a hateful action

1. **Odium** could be felt for the man who destroyed the school.
2. Shunned by the community, her **odium** made her an outcast.

A54

adj.—1. excessive; 2. unnecessary

1. Only the first sentence is necessary; all of these details are **superfluous**.
2. After they finished their seven-course meal, a large dessert seemed **superfluous**.

Questions

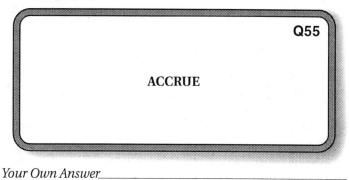

Q55

ACCRUE

*Your Own Answer*_____

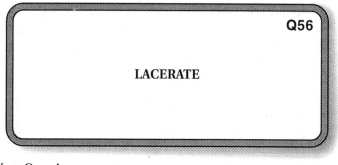

Q56

LACERATE

*Your Own Answer*_____

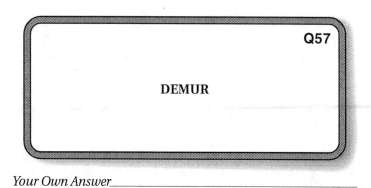

Q57

DEMUR

*Your Own Answer*_____

Correct Answers

A55

v.—1. to come to a person or thing by way of gain or increment; 2. to increase through natural growth

1. Over the course of her college career, she managed to **accrue** a great deal of knowledge.
2. Regular deposits enabled her to **accrue** a sizable savings account.

A56

v.—1. to tear or mangle; 2. to wound or hurt

1. Sharp knives may **lacerate** the skin of an unsuspecting user.
2. Her rejection will **lacerate** my self-esteem.

A57

1: v.; 2. n.—1. to hesitate due to doubts; 2. an objection raised

1. She **demurred** her decision to jump into the water when she thought she saw a shark.
2. While the defense attorney cross-examined the witness, the prosecutor stood up and offered a **demur**.

Questions

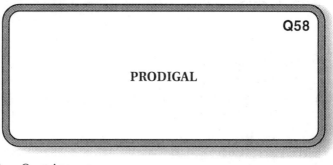

Q58

PRODIGAL

*Your Own Answer*_____

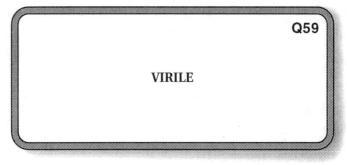

Q59

VIRILE

*Your Own Answer*_____

Q60

IGNOMINIOUS

*Your Own Answer*_____

Correct Answers

A58

adj.—1. wasteful; 2. generous

1. Spending all of your salary on expensive items is **prodigal**.
2. The **prodigal** gift by the poor woman was truly a thoughtful gesture.

A59

adj.—masculine; manly

Strong muscles and wide shoulders are only a few characteristics that identify him as a **virile** young man.

A60

adj.—1. contemptible; disgraceful; 2. degrading

1. The behavior was so **ignominious** he was ashamed to be associated with it.
2. She left him because of his **ignominious** treatment of her.

Questions

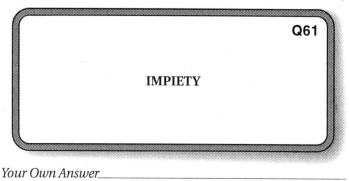

Q61

IMPIETY

*Your Own Answer*_____

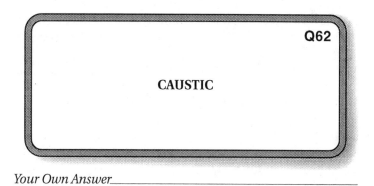

Q62

CAUSTIC

*Your Own Answer*_____

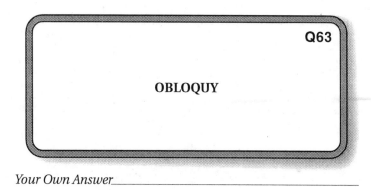

Q63

OBLOQUY

*Your Own Answer*_____

Correct Answers

A61

n.—1. irreverence toward God; 2. lack of respect

1. The bishop condemned the **impiety** of the celebrity's assertions.
2. **Impiety** is evident in the way many people commit rude actions.

A62

adj.—1. eating away at; 2. sarcastic words

1. The **caustic** chemicals are dangerous.
2. The girl harmed her mother with her **caustic** remarks.

A63

n.—verbal condemnation or abuse of a person or thing

The child suffered **obloquy** at the hands of his classmates.

Questions

IMPLICIT

*Your Own Answer*_____

COLLOQUIAL

*Your Own Answer*_____

PROBLEMATIC

*Your Own Answer*_____

Correct Answers

adj.—1. understood but not plainly stated; 2. without doubt

1. The child's anger was **implicit**.
2. **Implicit** trust must be earned.

adj.—1. having to do with conversation; 2. informal speech

1. The **colloquial** reference indicated the free spirit of the group.
2. When you listen to **colloquial** language in a written work, you realize how good an ear a novelist must have to write authentic dialogue.

adj.—1. being hard to deal with; 2. unsolved situation

1. The constant squeak of the door was **problematic**.
2. The tense political struggle remains **problematic**.

Questions

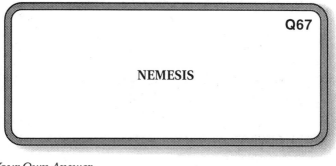

Q67

NEMESIS

*Your Own Answer*_____

_____

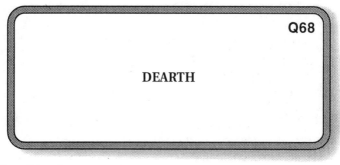

Q68

DEARTH

*Your Own Answer*_____

_____

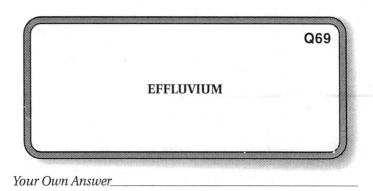

Q69

EFFLUVIUM

*Your Own Answer*_____

_____

Correct Answers

A67

n.—1. a person who inflicts just punishment; 2. a rival

1. The criminal was killed by his **nemesis**, the brother of the man he murdered.
2. The football team plays its **nemesis** on Saturday.

A68

n.—1. costliness; 2. scarcity of food

1. The **dearth** of the coverage forced him to look for a new insurance agent.
2. The floods and fire caused a **dearth** throughout the land.

A69

n.—1. an outflow of vapor of invisible particles; 2. a noxious odor

1. The **effluvium** from the exhaust had a bad smell.
2. It was difficult to determine the source of the **effluvium**.

Questions

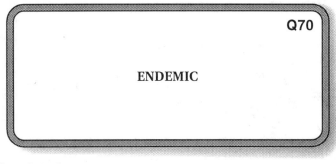

Q70

ENDEMIC

*Your Own Answer*_____

_____

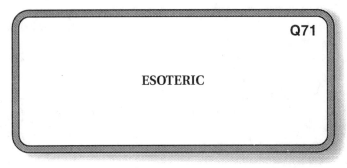

Q71

ESOTERIC

*Your Own Answer*_____

_____

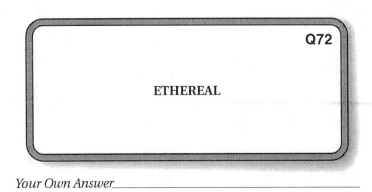

Q72

ETHEREAL

*Your Own Answer*_____

_____

Correct Answers

A70

adj.—1. native to a particular area; 2. constantly present in a particular country or locality

1. The **endemic** fauna was of great interest to the scientist.
2. A fast-paced style is **endemic** to those who live in New York City.

A71

adj.—1. understood by only a chosen few; 2. confidential

1. The **esoteric** language was only known by the select group.
2. We have had a number of **esoteric** conversations.

A72

adj.—1. very light; airy; 2. heavenly; not earthly

1. The **ethereal** quality of the music had a hypnotic effect.
2. After the lights went out in the planetarium, the room had an **ethereal** atmosphere.

Questions

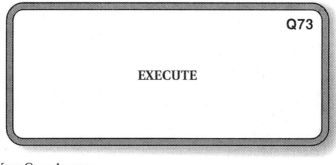

Q73

EXECUTE

*Your Own Answer*_____

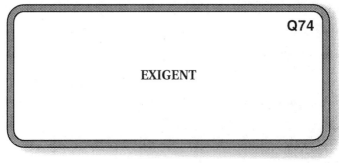

Q74

EXIGENT

*Your Own Answer*_____

Q75

TRAVAIL

*Your Own Answer*_____

Correct Answers

v.—1. to put to death; kill; 2. to carry out; fulfill

1. Some historians feel that Sacco and Vanzetti were **executed** for their political beliefs, rather than any wrongdoing.
2. I expected him to **execute** my orders immediately.

adj.—1. calling for immediate attention; 2. needing more than is reasonable

1. The **exigent** request for more assistance was answered quickly.
2. The bank seemed to feel that another extension on their loan payment was too **exigent** a request to honor.

n.—1. very hard work; 2. intense pain or agony

1. The farmer was tired after the **travail** of plowing the fields.
2. The aspirin finally ended her **travail**.

Questions

FASTIDIOUS

*Your Own Answer*_____

FATUOUS

*Your Own Answer*_____

FEINT

*Your Own Answer*_____

Correct Answers

A76

adj.—1. difficult to please; 2. excessive care or delicacy; painstaking

1. The **fastidious** girl would not accept any offers as suitable.

2. The woman was extremely **fastidious**, as evident in the long hours she would take to complete a minor task.

A77

adj.—1. lacking in seriousness; 2. vain and silly

1. The **fatuous** prank was meant to add comedy to the situation.

2. His **fatuous** personality demands that he stop in front of every mirror.

A78

1. v.; 2. n.—1. to pretend to throw a punch, as in boxing; 2. a fake show intended to deceive

1. The fighter **feinted** a left hook just before he went for the knockout.

2. His air of approval was a **feint** to hide his real motives.

Questions

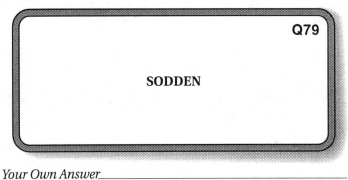

Q79

SODDEN

*Your Own Answer*_____

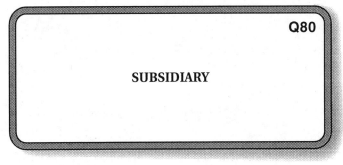

Q80

SUBSIDIARY

*Your Own Answer*_____

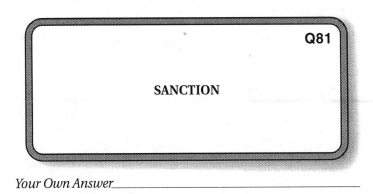

Q81

SANCTION

*Your Own Answer*_____

Correct Answers

A79

adj.—1. soggy; 2. dull in action as if from alcohol

1. The flowers were **sodden** after the rain.
2. The **sodden** reaction of the man caused the accident.

A80

adj.—1. giving a service; 2. being in a subordinate position

1. The function of the **subsidiary** was to oversee the bank's commercial loans.
2. The **subsidiary** position of the man was to aid the President.

A81

v.—1. to give authoritative permission; 2. to penalize by way of discipline

1. The government has **sanctioned** the meetings as a worthy cause.
2. Economic **sanctions** were imposed upon the hostile country before troops were mobilized.

Questions

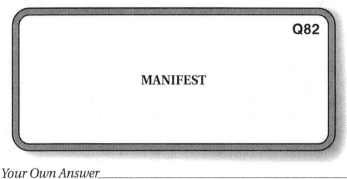

Q82

MANIFEST

*Your Own Answer*_____

_____

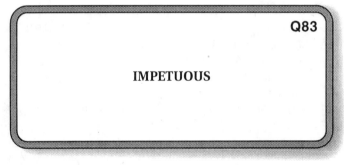

Q83

IMPETUOUS

*Your Own Answer*_____

_____

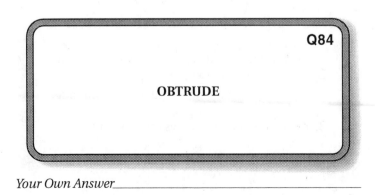

Q84

OBTRUDE

*Your Own Answer*_____

_____

Correct Answers

A82

v.—1. to show clearly; 2. to appear

1. He **manifested** his love for her by kissing her cheek.
2. The color green should **manifest** itself when yellow and blue are combined.

A83

adj.—1. moving with great force; 2. characterized by a sudden or rash action

1. The **impetuous** winds blew the picnic table into the neighbor's yard.
2. The **impetuous** leader fired all of his advisors when he thought they were plotting against him.

A84

v.—1. to force oneself or one's ideas upon another; 2. to thrust forward; to eject

1. She is very opinionated and always **obtrudes** upon others' conversations.
2. The man's belly **obtrudes** over his belt.

Questions

Q85

IGNOBLE

*Your Own Answer*_____

Q86

LAGGARD

*Your Own Answer*_____

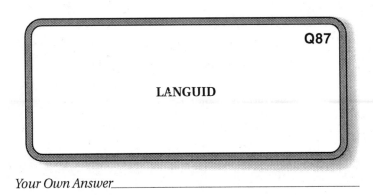

Q87

LANGUID

*Your Own Answer*_____

Correct Answers

A85

adj.—1. ordinary; 2. dishonorable

1. The king was adamant about keeping his daughter from wedding an **ignoble** man.
2. Consciously lying to someone is **ignoble**.

A86

1. n.; 2. adj.—1. a person who has fallen behind; 2. moving slowly

1. The **laggard** with the broken leg could not catch up with the tour group.
2. The **laggard** train was one hour late because there was a problem with the engine.

A87

adj.—1. lacking vitality; 2. indifferent

1. The **languid** student was always late to class.
2. I have studied so much that I have grown **languid** to the subject.

Questions

Q88

HAGGARD

*Your Own Answer*_____

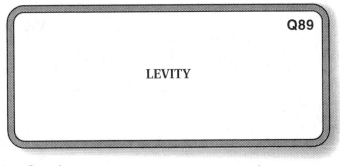

Q89

LEVITY

*Your Own Answer*_____

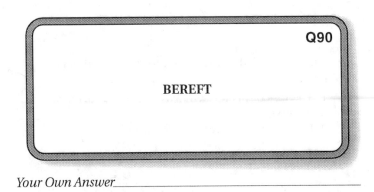

Q90

BEREFT

*Your Own Answer*_____

Correct Answers

A88

adj.—1. untamed; 2. having a worn look

1. The uncut lawn in front of the abandoned house added to its **haggard** look.

2. He looked as **haggard** as you would expect a new father of quadruplets to look.

A89

n.—1. lack of seriousness; 2. instability

1. He approached his job with such **levity** that he was demoted.

2. **Levity** characterized the first months of his administration.

A90

adj.—1. to be deprived of; 2. to be in a sad manner

1. The loss of his job will leave the man **bereft** of many luxuries.

2. He was **bereft** over the loss of his pet.

Questions

Q91

REPUDIATE

*Your Own Answer*_____

_____

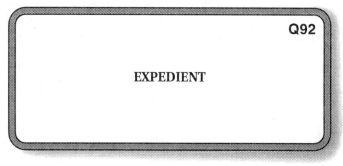

Q92

EXPEDIENT

*Your Own Answer*_____

_____

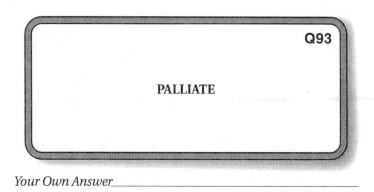

Q93

PALLIATE

*Your Own Answer*_____

_____

Correct Answers

v.—1. to disown; 2. to deny support for

1. The man will **repudiate** all claims that he was involved in the deal.
2. Although his party supported the bill, this senator **repudiated** it.

adj.—1. convenient in obtaining a result; 2. guided by self-interest

1. The mayor chose the more **expedient** path rather than the more correct one.
2. There is no **expedient** method a teenager will not resort to in order to get the keys to a car of his/her own.

v.—1. to alleviate or ease pain but not cure; 2. to make appear less serious

1. The medication will help **palliate** the pain.
2. The lawyer attempted to **palliate** the offense to the jury.

Questions

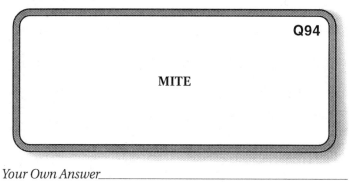

Q94

MITE

*Your Own Answer*_____

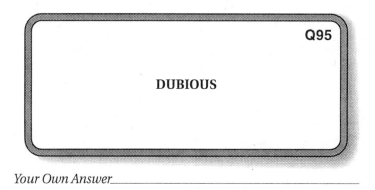

Q95

DUBIOUS

*Your Own Answer*_____

Q96

TEEM

*Your Own Answer*_____

Correct Answers

n.—1. a very small sum of money; 2. a very small creature

1. The **mite** they pay me is hardly worth the aggravation.
2. The baseball team was made up of such small children they were nicknamed the "**Mites**."

adj.—1. causing doubt; 2. hesitating; 3. an undecided outcome

1. The new information was **dubious** enough to re-open the case.
2. Her **dubious** objections went unheeded.
3. Too close to call, the outcome of the fight remains somewhat **dubious**.

v.—1. to be stocked to overflowing; 2. to pour out; to empty

1. The new plant seemed to be **teeming** with insects.
2. I **teemed** the excess oil from the pan.

Questions

Q97

NOISOME

*Your Own Answer*_____

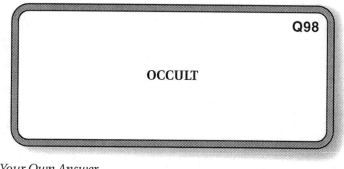

Q98

OCCULT

*Your Own Answer*_____

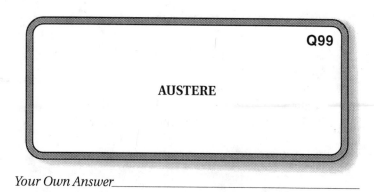

Q99

AUSTERE

*Your Own Answer*_____

Correct Answers

A97

adj.—1. harmful to health; 2. having a foul odor

1. The **noisome** food was the cause of their illness.
2. The family was forced from the home by a **noisome** odor.

A98

1. adj.; 2. n.—1. mysterious, beyond the range of ordinary knowledge; 2. supernatural agencies and affairs considered as a whole

1. The **occult** meaning of the message was one of dislike for the authorities.
2. There will be a documentary on television tonight about various sects of the **occult**.

A99

adj.—1. having a stern look; 2. having strict self-discipline

1. The old woman always has an **austere** look about her.
2. The headmaster was known as an **austere** teacher.

Questions

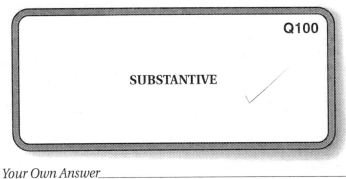

Q100

SUBSTANTIVE

*Your Own Answer*_____

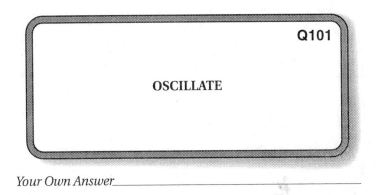

Q101

OSCILLATE

*Your Own Answer*_____

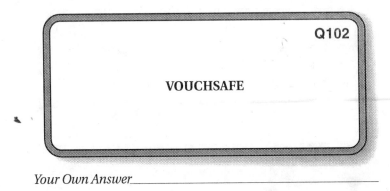

Q102

VOUCHSAFE

*Your Own Answer*_____

Correct Answers

A100

adj.—1. existing independently of others; 2. a large quantity; 3. essential

1. The only company not acquired in the merger retained its **substantive** existence.
2. A **substantive** amount of money will be needed to fund the project.
3. Having good credit is **substantive** when applying for a loan.

A101

v.—1. to move back and forth; 2. to have a wavering opinion

1. The **oscillating** sprinkler system covered the entire lawn.
2. The couple often **oscillates** between going out and staying home.

A102

v.—1. to grant or give, as by favor or graciousness; 2. to allow or permit

1. The owner of the property agreed to **vouchsafe** our use of her land.
2. They **vouchsafed** his return to his own country.

Questions

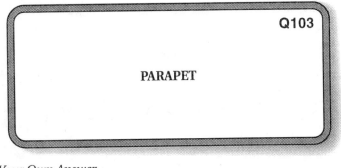

Q103

PARAPET

*Your Own Answer*_____

_____

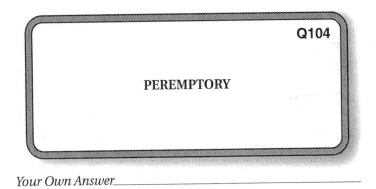

Q104

PEREMPTORY

*Your Own Answer*_____

_____

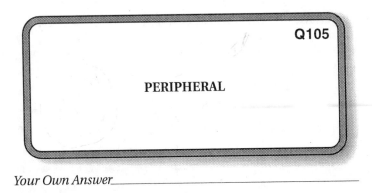

Q105

PERIPHERAL

*Your Own Answer*_____

_____

Correct Answers

n.—1. a wall for protection; 2. a low wall or railing

1. The **parapet** protected the kingdom from the raging army.

2. The **parapet** kept the child from falling into the river.

adj.—1. barring future action; 2. that which cannot be denied, or changed; final

1. A **peremptory** decision was made when a video showing the defendant's guilt was found.

2. The wildcat strike was a **peremptory** move on the part of the workers.

adj.—1. the outer part of; 2. slightly connected to what is important

1. The **peripheral** arrangement of the shrubs was used to create a fence-like blockade.

2. His paper was filled with **peripheral** comments, and never dealt with the main argument.

Questions

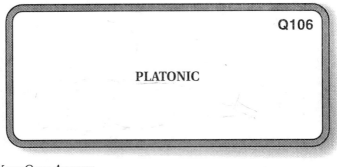

Q106

PLATONIC

*Your Own Answer*_____

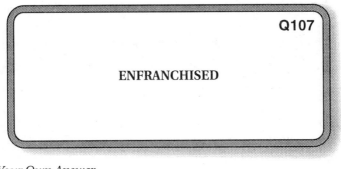

Q107

ENFRANCHISED

*Your Own Answer*_____

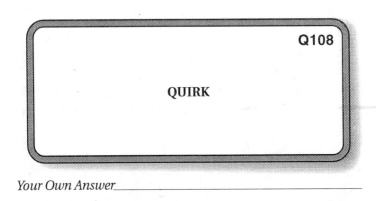

Q108

QUIRK

*Your Own Answer*_____

Correct Answers

A106

adj.—1. of, pertaining to, or characteristic of Plato's philosophy;
2. not amorous or sensual

1. In class we spoke about the **platonic** philosophy of ideal forms.
2. Our relationship is **platonic** now, but I hope it will someday be otherwise.

A107

v.—1. to free from obligation; 2. to admit to citizenship

1. The player was **enfranchised** when the deal was called off.
2. The recent immigrants were **enfranchised** when they took their oath to their new country.

A108

n.— 1. a twist; 2. a peculiar trait

1. The plot of that movie had so many **quirks** that it became very hard to follow.
2. Always needing to put the left shoe on first is a **quirk**.

Questions

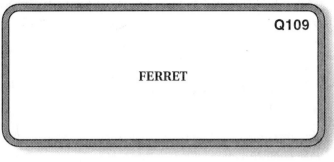

Q109

FERRET

*Your Own Answer*_____

_____

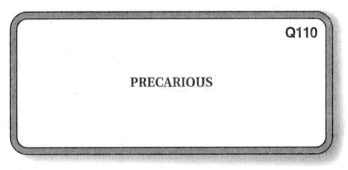

Q110

PRECARIOUS

*Your Own Answer*_____

_____

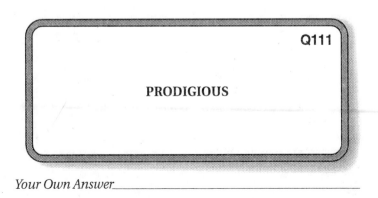

Q111

PRODIGIOUS

*Your Own Answer*_____

_____

Correct Answers

A109

1. v.; 2. v.; 3. n.—1. to force out of hiding; 2. to search for; 3. a small, weasel-like mammal

1. The police will **ferret** the fugitive out of his hiding place.
2. I spent the morning **ferreting** for my keys.
3. I have a pet **ferret**.

A110

adj.—1. depending upon another; 2. risky; uncertain

1. I will have to check the weather forecast because my plans are **precarious** upon the weather.
2. My position in the negotiations was **precarious** at best.

A111

adj.—1. wonderful; 2. enormous

1. The **prodigious** festivities lasted until the wee hours of the morning.
2. The new skyscraper was a **prodigious** addition to the skyline.

Questions

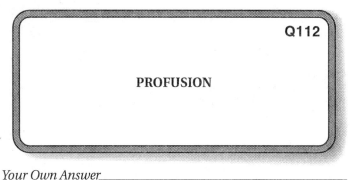

Q112

PROFUSION

*Your Own Answer*_____

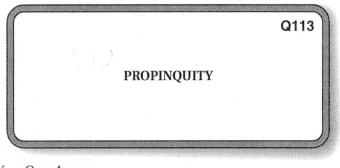

Q113

PROPINQUITY

*Your Own Answer*_____

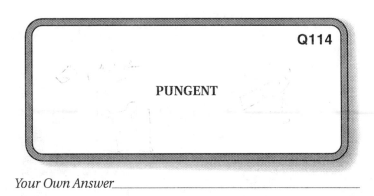

Q114

PUNGENT

*Your Own Answer*_____

Correct Answers

A112

n.—1. great wastefulness; 2. a large abundance

1. The **profusion** of the food fight was unforgivable considering the worldwide hunger problem.
2. The **profusion** of uneaten food was sent to the shelter.

A113

n.—1. closeness in time or place; 2. closeness of relationship

1. The **propinquity** of the disasters put the community in chaos.
2. The **propinquity** of the two stories was the basis of the teacher's lesson.

A114

adj.—1. sharp and piercing; 2. expressive

1. The **pungent** smell of cheese cut through the sweet smell of grapes.
2. Her **pungent** words brought a tear to her eye.

Questions

Q115

HARBOR

*Your Own Answer*_____

_____

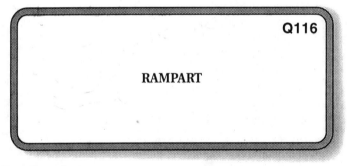

Q116

RAMPART

*Your Own Answer*_____

_____

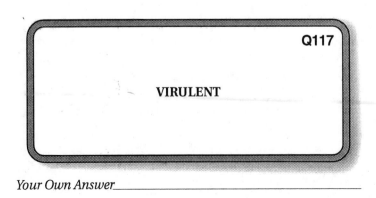

Q117

VIRULENT

*Your Own Answer*_____

_____

Correct Answers

A115

1. n.; 2. v.—1. a place of safety or shelter; 2. to give shelter or protect

1. The rabbits used the shed as a **harbor** from the raging storm.
2. Her decision to **harbor** a known criminal was an unwise one.

A116

1. n.; 2. v.—1. a defense; 2. to defend

1. The **rampart** the soldiers built was severely damaged and they had no more protection from the enemy.
2. The soldiers will attempt to **rampart** the castle.

A117

adj.—1. poisonous; 2. full of hate

1. The rattlesnake's **virulent** bite demanded medical attention.
2. Her **virulent** and racist remarks were the result of years of hatred.

Questions

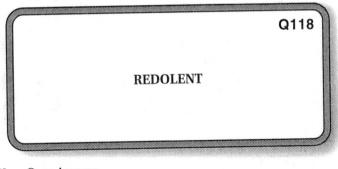

Q118

REDOLENT

*Your Own Answer*_____

_____

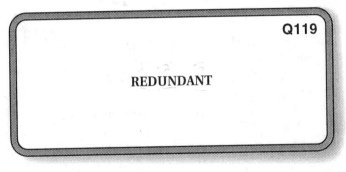

Q119

REDUNDANT

*Your Own Answer*_____

_____

Q120

INNOCUOUS

*Your Own Answer*_____

_____

Correct Answers

A118

adj.—sweet-smelling
The restaurant was **redolent** with spices.

A119

adj.—1. wordy; repetitive; 2. unnecessary to the meaning

1. The **redundant** lecture of the professor repeated the lesson in the text.
2. Her comments were both **redundant** and sarcastic.

A120

adj.—1. harmless; 2. dull

1. The remark was rude but **innocuous**.
2. He couldn't bear to sit through another **innocuous** lecture.

Questions

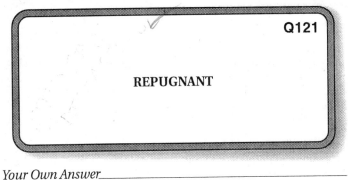

Q121

REPUGNANT

*Your Own Answer*_____

_____

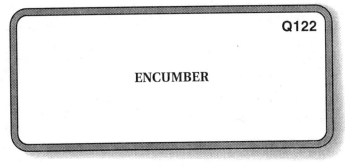

Q122

ENCUMBER

*Your Own Answer*_____

_____

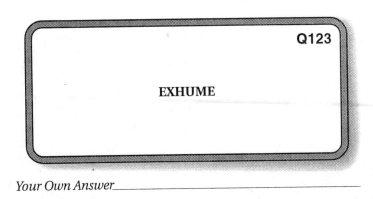

Q123

EXHUME

*Your Own Answer*_____

_____

Correct Answers

A121

adj.—1. distasteful; offensive; 2. opposed to

1. The **repugnant** actions of the man made others lose trust in him.
2. Despite their efforts to convince her, she remained **repugnant**.

A122

v.—1. to hold back; to hinder; 2. to burden; load down

1. The review of the ethics committee **encumbered** the deal from being finalized.
2. A brace will **encumber** the girl's movement.

A123

v.—1. to unearth; 2. to reveal

1. The scientists **exhumed** the body from the grave to test the body's DNA.
2. The next episode will **exhume** the real betrayer.

Questions

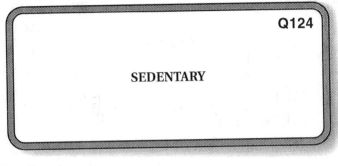

Q124

SEDENTARY

*Your Own Answer*_____

_____

Q125

SEDULOUS

*Your Own Answer*_____

_____

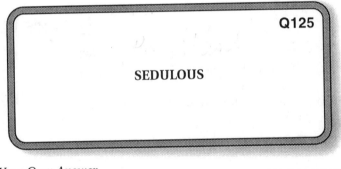

Q126

FLAG

*Your Own Answer*_____

_____

Correct Answers

adj.—1. characterized by sitting; 2. remaining in one locality

1. The **sedentary** child had not moved for two hours.
2. The old woman, who never left her hometown, has led a **sedentary** life.

adj.—1. working diligently; 2. persistent

1. The **sedulous** habits of the team will surely conclude in victory.
2. Only the most **sedulous** salespeople will succeed.

v.—1. to become weak; 2. to send a message

1. The smaller animal **flagged** before the larger one.
2. The stranded motorist will attempt to **flag** down help with a flare.

Questions

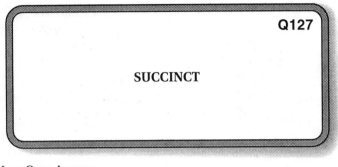

Q127

SUCCINCT

*Your Own Answer*_____

_____

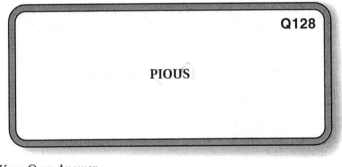

Q128

PIOUS

*Your Own Answer*_____

_____

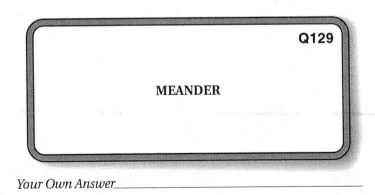

Q129

MEANDER

*Your Own Answer*_____

_____

Correct Answers

adj.—1. clearly stated; 2. characterized by conciseness

1. The speech was **succinct** yet emotional.
2. Usually, the most **succinct** definition is the right one.

adj.—1. having a religious devotion; 2. sacred

1. The **pious** saints devoted their lives to serving God.
2. The Bible is considered to contain **pious** literature.

1. v.; 2. adj.—1. to wind; to wander; 2. winding; wandering aimlessly

1. The stream **meanders** through the valley.
2. Because we took a long, **meandering** walk, we arrived home well after dark.

Questions

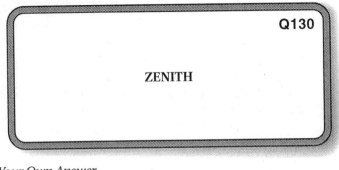

Q130

ZENITH

*Your Own Answer*_____

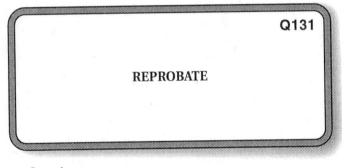

Q131

REPROBATE

*Your Own Answer*_____

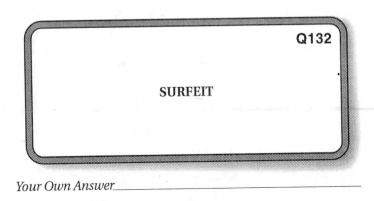

Q132

SURFEIT

*Your Own Answer*_____

Correct Answers

A130

n.—1. the point directly above in the sky; 2. the highest point

1. The sun will reach its **zenith** at noon.
2. The **zenith** of her career occurred during her time as chairperson.

A131

v.—1. to condemn; 2. to reject

1. The teacher will **reprobate** the actions of the delinquent student.
2. His assertions were **reprobated** as inappropriate.

A132

1. v.; 2. n.—1. to indulge excessively; 2. overindulgence

1. The teenagers were warned not to **surfeit** at the party.
2. The result of her **surfeit** was a week of regret.

Questions

Q133

DIFFUSE

*Your Own Answer*_____

Q134

TUMID

*Your Own Answer*_____

Q135

TUMULT

*Your Own Answer*_____

Correct Answers

A133

adj.—1. spread out; 2. wordy; not focused

1. The wind caused the dandelion seeds to fall in a **diffuse** manner.
2. Although the student's ideas were brilliant, they were obscured by her **diffuse** writing.

A134

adj.—1. swollen; 2. pompous

1. The **tumid** river washed away the homes built on the shore.
2. After he earned his doctorate, he became insufferably **tumid**.

A135

n.—1. a noisy commotion; 2. disturbance

1. The **tumult** was caused by two boys wanting the same toy.
2. After the **tumult**, I found it difficult to resume my studies.

Questions

PLUMB

*Your Own Answer*_____

Q137

GAMUT

*Your Own Answer*_____

Q138

VENEER

*Your Own Answer*_____

Correct Answers

1. adj.; 2. v.—1. perfectly straight down; 2. to solve

1.The ruler made two vertical, **plumb** lines on the graph paper.

2. I was able to **plumb** the riddle in a few seconds.

n.—1. a complete range; 2. any complete musical scale

1. The woman's wardrobe runs the **gamut** from jeans to suits.

2. His first composition covered the entire **gamut** of the major scale.

n.—1. a thin surface layer; 2. any attractive but superficial appearance

1. The **veneer** was peeling off the counter.

2. Her **veneer** of honesty covered her lies.

Questions

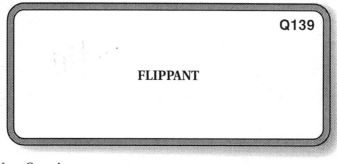

Q139

FLIPPANT

*Your Own Answer*_____

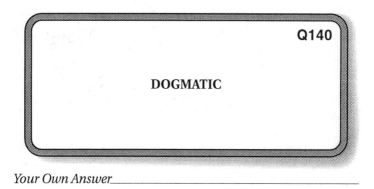

Q140

DOGMATIC

*Your Own Answer*_____

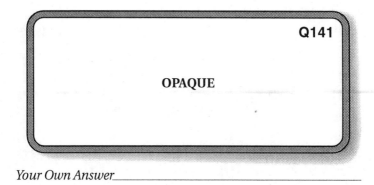

Q141

OPAQUE

*Your Own Answer*_____

Correct Answers

adj.—1. talkative; 2. disrespectful

1. The youngsters were **flippant** in the restaurant.
2. The teacher became upset with the **flippant** answer from the student.

adj.—1. of a belief; 2. suggested without proof; 3. making assertions with an arrogant manner

1. Their **dogmatic** declaration clarified their position.
2. The **dogmatic** statement had not yet been proven by science.
3. The student's **dogmatic** presentation annoyed his classmates as well as his instructor.

adj.—1. dull or dark; 2. not allowing light to pass through

1. They chose an **opaque** shade of green for their bathroom walls.
2. All light was shut out of the room by the **opaque** shades.

Questions

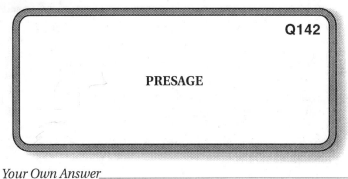

Q142

PRESAGE

*Your Own Answer*_____

_____

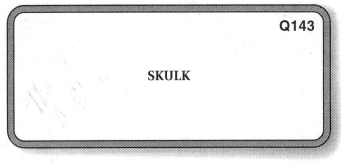

Q143

SKULK

*Your Own Answer*_____

_____

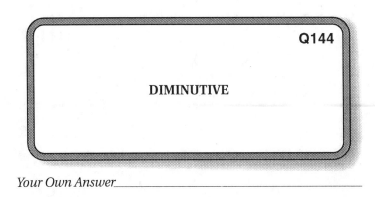

Q144

DIMINUTIVE

*Your Own Answer*_____

_____

Correct Answers

n.—1. an omen; 2. a foreshadowing characteristic
1. They considered the rainbow at their wedding a **presage** for a happy life.
2. Bright sun in the morning was a **presage** that it was going to be a good day.

v.—1. to move in a stealthy way; 2. to avoid responsibility
1. They found the boy **skulking** in the bushes.
2. The woman attempted to **skulk** away from cleaning the house by hiring a cleaning service.

adj.— smaller than average
A booklet is a **diminutive** form of a book.

Questions

Q145

SUNDRY

*Your Own Answer*_____

Q146

DEFERENCE

*Your Own Answer*_____

Q147

JETTISON

*Your Own Answer*_____

Correct Answers

adj.—1. various; miscellaneous; 2. separate; distinct

1. This store sells **sundry** items.
2. The author waited to hand out his book about different religions to a **sundry** audience.

n.—1. a yielding of opinion; 2. courteous respect for

1. To avoid a confrontation, the man showed **deference** to his friend.
2. The **deference** shown to the elderly woman's opinion was heartwarming.

v.—1. to throw goods overboard to lighten a vehicle; 2. to discard

1. To raise the balloon above the storm clouds, they had to **jettison** the ballast.
2. When he was through eating the banana, he **jettisoned** the peel.

Questions

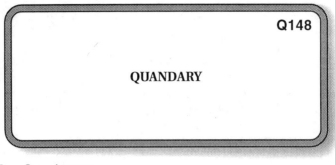

Q148

QUANDARY

*Your Own Answer*_____

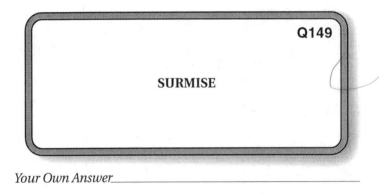

Q149

SURMISE

*Your Own Answer*_____

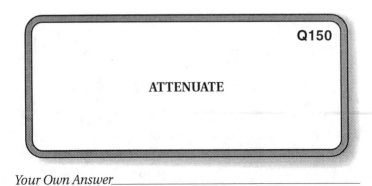

Q150

ATTENUATE

*Your Own Answer*_____

Correct Answers

A148

n.—1. a state of uncertainty; 2. difficult situation

1. Unable to make a firm decision, I've been in this **quandary** for weeks.
2. When the car broke down the commuter was left in a **quandary**.

A149

1. n.; 2. v.—1. a guess; 2. to guess

1. Was my **surmise** correct?
2. I **surmise** that we will not arrive at the party on time.

A150

1. v.; 2. adj.—1. to thin out; 2. weakened; diminishing

1. Water is commonly used to **attenuate** strong chemicals.
2. A vaccine often contains an **attenuated** form of the virus it is designed to prevent.

Questions

Q151

RIVET

*Your Own Answer*_____

_____

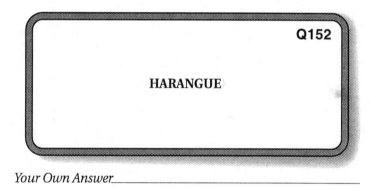

Q152

HARANGUE

*Your Own Answer*_____

_____

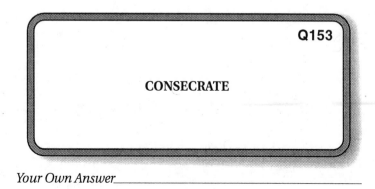

Q153

CONSECRATE

*Your Own Answer*_____

_____

Correct Answers

v.—1. to secure; 2. to hold firmly or to be engrossed

1. We can **rivet** the boat to the dock.
2. She could not look away from the morbid scene; she was **riveted** to it.

1. n.; 2. v.—1. a lengthy, heartfelt speech; 2. to talk excitedly

1. We sat patiently and listened to her **harangue**.
2. When he finally stopped **haranguing**, I responded calmly.

v.—1. to declare sacred; 2. to dedicate

1. We will **consecrate** the pact during the ceremony.
2. The park was **consecrated** to the memory of the missing soldier.

Questions

Q154

TORPID

*Your Own Answer*_____

Q155

RABID

*Your Own Answer*_____

Q156

TENACIOUS

*Your Own Answer*_____

Correct Answers

adj.—1. being dormant; 2. slow, sluggish

1. When we came upon the hibernating bear, it was in a **torpid** state.

2. A **torpid** animal does not act with energy.

adj.—1. violent; 2. fanatic about a belief

1. With a **rabid** outburst, the man left the room where he had just been fired.

2. He's been a **rabid** sports fan for as long as I have known him.

adj.—1. holding firmly; 2. persistent

1. With a **tenacious** grip, the man was finally able to pull the nail from the wall.

2. After his **tenacious** pleas, she finally conceded.

Questions

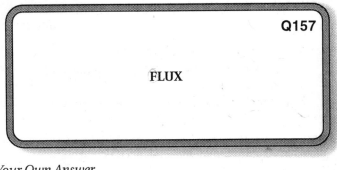

Q157

FLUX

*Your Own Answer*_____

_____

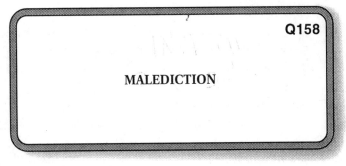

Q158

MALEDICTION

*Your Own Answer*_____

_____

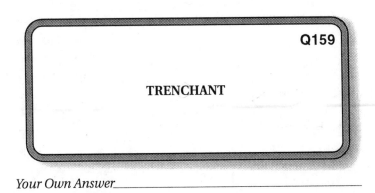

Q159

TRENCHANT

*Your Own Answer*_____

_____

Correct Answers

A157

n.—1. a flow; 2. a continual change

1. With the **flux** of new students into the school, space was limited.

2. The price of gasoline is in a state of **flux**.

A158

n.—1. putting a curse on someone; 2. talking negatively about another

1. With the threat of a **malediction**, the man left the fortuneteller's house.

2. Her conversations are full of **malediction**.

A159

adj.—1. cutting; 2. keen or incisive

1. Without a **trenchant** tool, they would have to break off the branches.

2. The **trenchant** words hurt the man deeply.

Questions

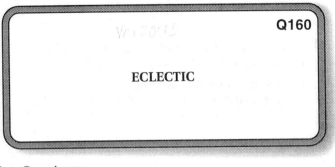

ECLECTIC

*Your Own Answer*_____

_____

Q161

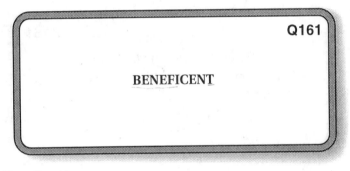

BENEFICENT

*Your Own Answer*_____

_____

Q162

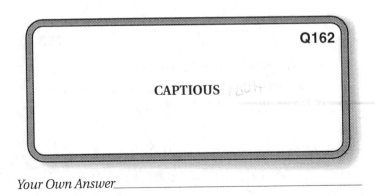

CAPTIOUS

*Your Own Answer*_____

_____

Correct Answers

A160

adj.—1. picking from various possibilities; 2. made up of material from various sources
1. You have **eclectic** taste.
2. The **eclectic** collection of furniture did not match.

A161

adj.—conferring benefits; kindly; doing good
A **beneficent** donation helped the organization meet its goal.

A162

adj.—disposed to find fault
A **captious** attitude often causes difficulties in a relationship.

Questions

CIRCUMSPECT

*Your Own Answer*_____

_____

GUFFAW

*Your Own Answer*_____

_____

AMELIORATE

*Your Own Answer*_____

_____

Correct Answers

A163

adj.—considering all circumstances

A **circumspect** decision must be made when so many people are involved.

A164

n.—boisterous laughter

A comedian's success is assured when the audience gives forth a **guffaw** following his jokes.

A165

v.—to improve or make better

A consistent routine of exercise has been shown to **ameliorate** health.

Questions

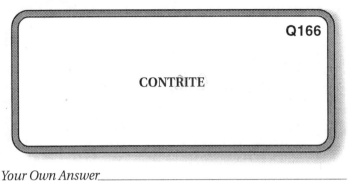

Q166

CONTRITE

*Your Own Answer*_____

_____

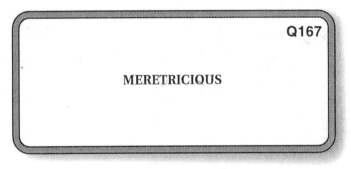

Q167

MERETRICIOUS

*Your Own Answer*_____

_____

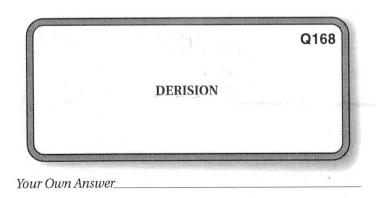

Q168

DERISION

*Your Own Answer*_____

_____

Correct Answers

adj.—repentant

A **contrite** heart has fixed its wrongs.

adj.—attractive by a show of flashy or vulgar qualities; tawdry

The **meretricious** girl tried to look like she was wealthy, but her fake gold jewelry revealed the truth.

n.—ridicule

A day of **derision** from the boss left the employee feeling depressed.

Questions

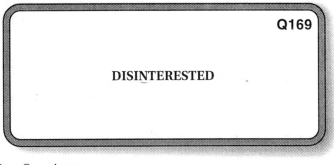

Q169

DISINTERESTED

*Your Own Answer*_____

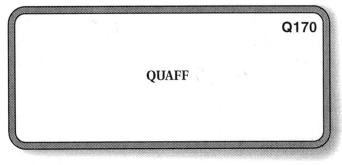

Q170

QUAFF

*Your Own Answer*_____

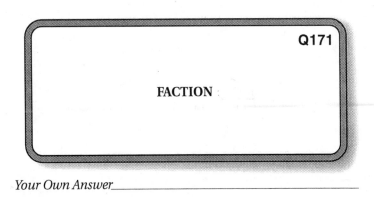

Q171

FACTION

*Your Own Answer*_____

Correct Answers

adj.—neutral; unbiased (alternate meaning: uninterested)

A **disinterested** person was needed to serve as arbitrator of the argument.

v.—to drink heartily

A dog will **quaff** if it becomes overheated.

n.—a number of people in an organization working for a common cause against the main body

A **faction** of the student body supported the president's view.

Questions

Q172

FETTER

*Your Own Answer*_____

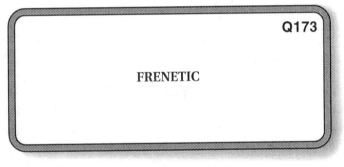

Q173

FRENETIC

*Your Own Answer*_____

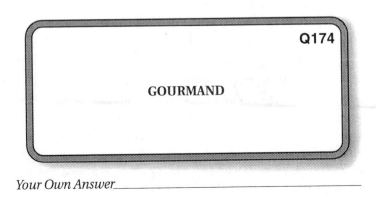

Q174

GOURMAND

*Your Own Answer*_____

Correct Answers

n.—a chain to bind the feet together
The prisoner was bound by handcuffs and **fetters**.

adj.—frenzied
A **frenetic** call was made from the crime scene.

n.—one who eats heartily
A **gourmand** may eat several servings of an entree.

Questions

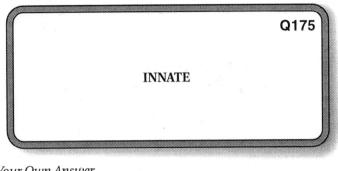

Q175

INNATE

*Your Own Answer*_____

_____

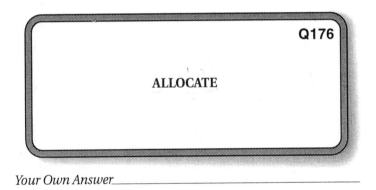

Q176

ALLOCATE

*Your Own Answer*_____

_____

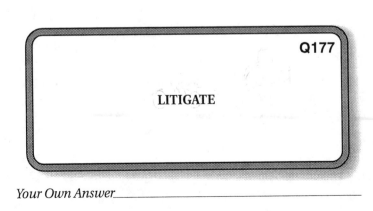

Q177

LITIGATE

*Your Own Answer*_____

_____

Correct Answers

A175

adj.—existing from birth
A lion's hunting skills are **innate**.

A176

v.—to set aside; to designate; to assign
A number of front-row seats were **allocated** to the performers' families and the top givers.

A177

v.—to involve a lawsuit
A number of the state attorneys-general are **litigating** against the tobacco companies.

Questions

Q178

PAEAN

*Your Own Answer*_____

Q179

PARTISAN

*Your Own Answer*_____

Q180

QUIESCENCE

*Your Own Answer*_____

Correct Answers

A178

n.—a song of praise or triumph

A **paean** was written in honor of the victorious warrior.

A179

n.—a person who strongly supports one view

Jane is an avid **partisan** of the Democratic party, and will not vote for a Republican.

A180

n.—state of being at rest or without motion; stillness

A period of **quiescence** is useful to calm the nerves.

Questions

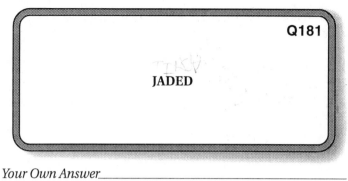

Q181

JADED

*Your Own Answer*_____

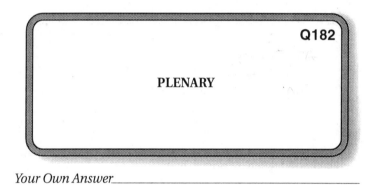

Q182

PLENARY

*Your Own Answer*_____

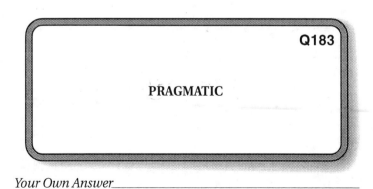

Q183

PRAGMATIC

*Your Own Answer*_____

Correct Answers

A181

adj.—worn-out

A person may become **jaded** if forced to work too many hours.

A182

adj.—full; entire; absolute

The leader exhibited **plenary** power when he over-ruled the unanimous decision made by his cabinet.

A183

adj.—practical

A **pragmatic** solution to continually repairing the car would be to purchase a new one.

Questions

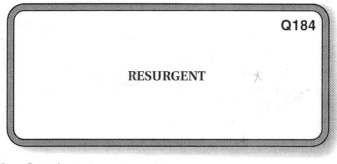

Q184

RESURGENT

Your Own Answer

Q185

SCRUPULOUS

Your Own Answer

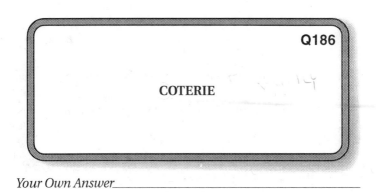

Q186

COTERIE

Your Own Answer

Correct Answers

A184

adj.—rising or tending to rise again

A **resurgent** wave of enthusiasm erupted from the once quiet crowd.

A185

adj.—making sure all details are perfect

A **scrupulous** cleaning was conducted before the family moved.

A186

n.— a clique; a group who meets frequently, usually socially

A special aspect of campus life is joining a **coterie**.

Questions

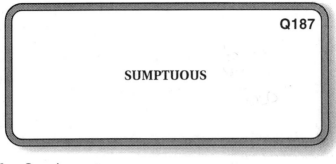

Q187

SUMPTUOUS

*Your Own Answer*_____

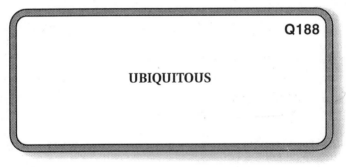

Q188

UBIQUITOUS

*Your Own Answer*_____

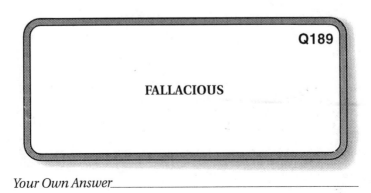

Q189

FALLACIOUS

*Your Own Answer*_____

Correct Answers

A187

adj.—involving great expense; splendid; lavish
When the Smiths won the lottery, they built a **sumptuous** new house.

A188

adj.—present everywhere
There was an **ubiquitous** sadness in the community after the tragedy.

A189

adj.—misleading; deceptive
A used car salesman provided **fallacious** information that caused the naive man to purchase the car.

Questions

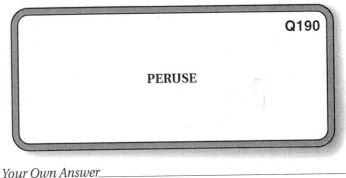

Q190

PERUSE

*Your Own Answer*_____

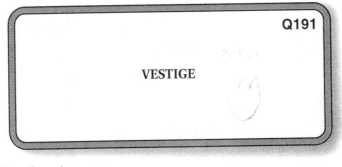

Q191

VESTIGE

*Your Own Answer*_____

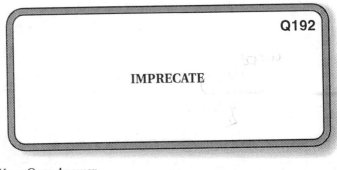

Q192

IMPRECATE

*Your Own Answer*_____

Correct Answers

A190

v.—to read carefully; to study

She spent days **perusing** her text books in preparation for her final exams.

A191

n.—a trace of something that no longer exists

A **vestige** of scent remained from the flower arrangement.

A192

v.—to pray for evil; to invoke a curse

A witch may **imprecate** an enemy with a curse of bad luck.

Questions

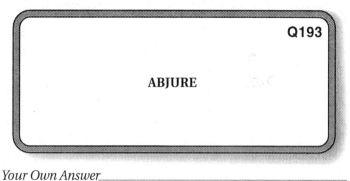

Q193

ABJURE

*Your Own Answer*_____

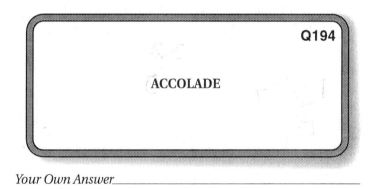

Q194

ACCOLADE

*Your Own Answer*_____

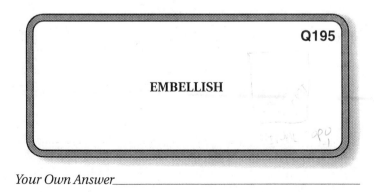

Q195

EMBELLISH

*Your Own Answer*_____

Correct Answers

A193

v.—to give up
Abjuring their oath to their king left the rebels open to charges of treason.

A194

n.—approving or praising mention
Accolades were showered on the returning hero.

A195

v.—to improve by adding details
Adding beads to a garment will **embellish** it.

Questions

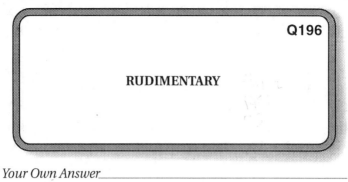

Q196

RUDIMENTARY

*Your Own Answer*_____

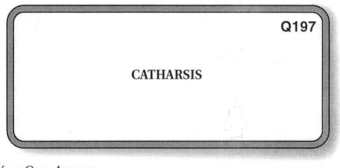

Q197

CATHARSIS

*Your Own Answer*_____

Q198

ALTRUISM

*Your Own Answer*_____

Correct Answers

A196

adj.—elementary
Adding two plus two is a **rudimentary** activity.

A197

n.—a purging or relieving of the body or soul
Admitting his guilt served as a **catharsis** for the man.

A198

n.— unselfish devotion to the welfare of others
Adversity can bring out **altruism** even among the jaded.

sparing

Questions

LACONIC

*Your Own Answer*_____

ABSTEMIOUS

*Your Own Answer*_____

DISHEARTENED

*Your Own Answer*_____

Correct Answers

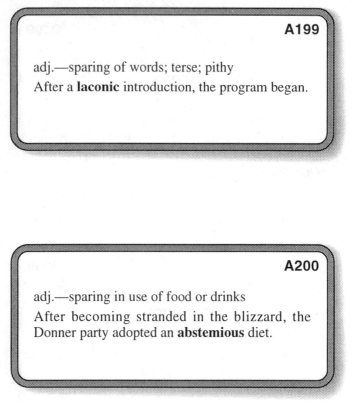

A199

adj.—sparing of words; terse; pithy

After a **laconic** introduction, the program began.

A200

adj.—sparing in use of food or drinks

After becoming stranded in the blizzard, the Donner party adopted an **abstemious** diet.

A201

adj.—discouraged; depressed

After failing the exam, the student became **disheartened** and wondered if he would ever graduate.

Questions

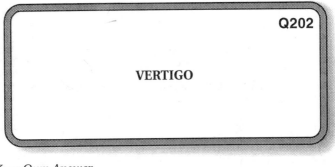

Q202

VERTIGO

*Your Own Answer*_____

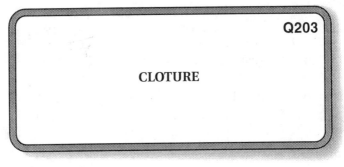

Q203

CLOTURE

*Your Own Answer*_____

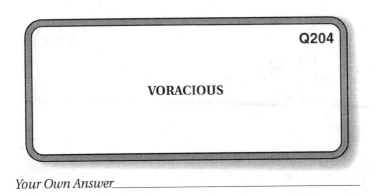

Q204

VORACIOUS

*Your Own Answer*_____

Correct Answers

A202

n.—a sensation of dizziness

After her car was hit from behind, the driver experienced **vertigo** when her head hit the steering wheel.

A203

n.—a parliamentary procedure to end debate and begin to vote

After hours of debate, the council began **cloture**.

A204

adj.—greedy in eating

After not eating for two days, the dog had a **voracious** appetite.

Questions

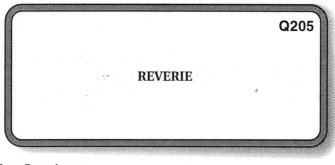

Q205

REVERIE

*Your Own Answer*_____

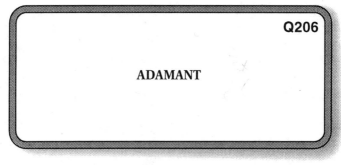

Q206

ADAMANT

*Your Own Answer*_____

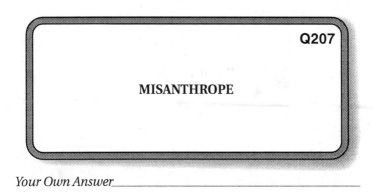

Q207

MISANTHROPE

*Your Own Answer*_____

Correct Answers

A205

n.—daydream

After spending the morning in **reverie**, I decided to work in the afternoon.

A206

adj.—not yielding, firm

After taking an **adamant** stand to sell the house himself, the man called the real estate agency to have it listed.

A207

n.—a person who hates or distrusts everything

After the man swindled the woman of her savings, she became a **misanthrope**.

Questions

Q208

FOSTER

*Your Own Answer*_____

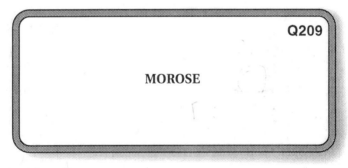

Q209

MOROSE

*Your Own Answer*_____

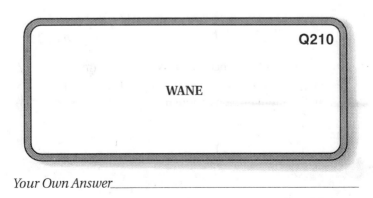

Q210

WANE

*Your Own Answer*_____

Correct Answers

A208

v.—encourage; nurture; support

After the severe storm, the gardener **fostered** many of his plants back to health.

A209

adj.—gloomy

After the team lost, the fans were **morose**.

A210

v.—to gradually become less; to grow dim

After time, interest in the show will **wane,** and it will no longer be as popular.

Questions

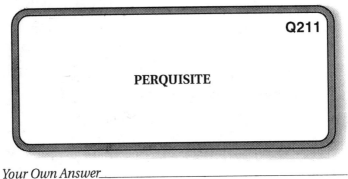

Q211

PERQUISITE

*Your Own Answer*_____

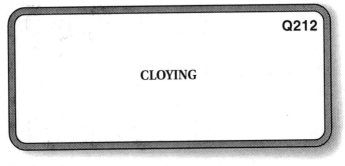

Q212

CLOYING

*Your Own Answer*_____

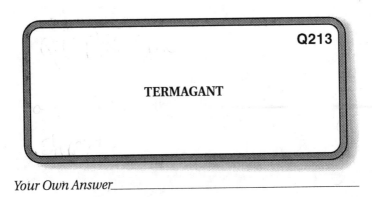

Q213

TERMAGANT

*Your Own Answer*_____

Correct Answers

A211

n.—a tip in addition to regular income
Every Christmas the generous company gave a
perquisite to its employees.

A212

adj.—causing disgust or aversion through excess
Every time she came over we held our noses because the **cloying** sweetness of her perfume made
us nauseous.

A213

n.—a constantly quarrelsome woman; a shrew
Agreement with the **termagant** was an impossi-
bility.

Questions

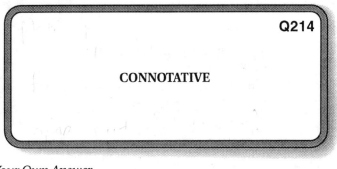

Q214

CONNOTATIVE

*Your Own Answer*_____

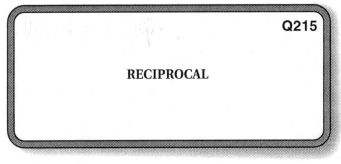

Q215

RECIPROCAL

*Your Own Answer*_____

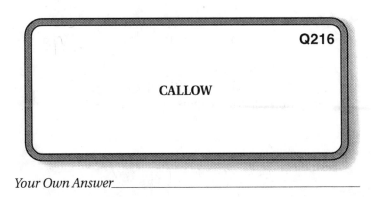

Q216

CALLOW

*Your Own Answer*_____

Correct Answers

A214

adj.—containing associated meanings in addition to the primary one

Along with the primary meaning of the word, there were two **connotative** meanings.

A215

n.—mutual; having the same relationship to each other

They realized their love was **reciprocal** when each received a valentine from the other.

A216

adj.—immature

Although the girl could be considered an adult, her action was very **callow**.

Questions

Q217

AMIABLE

*Your Own Answer*_____

Q218

KNAVERY

*Your Own Answer*_____

Q219

PARSE

*Your Own Answer*_____

Correct Answers

A217

adj.—friendly
Amiable and gregarious, Fred is bound to succeed.

A218

n.—a dishonest act
An act of **knavery** is cause for loss of trust.

A219

v.—to separate (a sentence) into parts and describe
the function of each
An English teacher may ask a student to **parse** a
sentence.

Questions

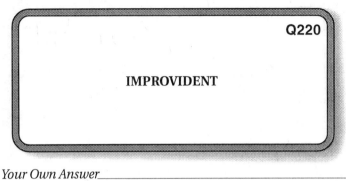

Q220

IMPROVIDENT

*Your Own Answer*_____

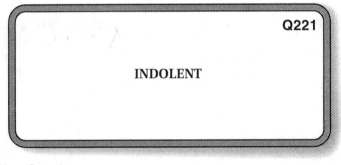

Q221

INDOLENT

*Your Own Answer*_____

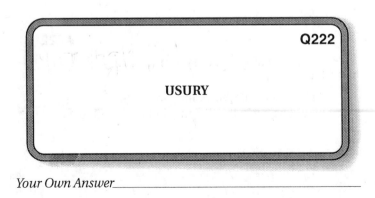

Q222

USURY

*Your Own Answer*_____

Correct Answers

adj.—not providing for the future

An **improvident** person may end up destitute later in life.

adj.—not wanting to work

An **indolent** student slept all day.

n.—the lending of money with an excessively high interest rate

An interest rate 30 points above the prime rate would be considered **usury** in the United States.

Questions

Q223

INTRACTABLE

Your Own Answer_____

Q224

UNALLOYED

Your Own Answer_____

Q225

ARTIFICE

Your Own Answer_____

Correct Answers

A223

adj.—stubborn; not easily taught or disciplined
An **intractable** pet can be very frustrating.

A224

adj.—pure, of high quality
An **unalloyed** chain is of greater value than a piece of costume jewelry.

A225

n.—an artful device
The **artifice** displayed by the actor made him the envy of many.

Questions

EPICURE

*Your Own Answer*_____

OBEISANCE

*Your Own Answer*_____

BANAL

*Your Own Answer*_____

Correct Answers

A226

n.—a person who has good taste in food and drink

An **epicure**, Lance is choosy about the restaurants he visits.

A227

n.—a gesture of respect or reverence

As an **obeisance**, the man took off his hat as the funeral procession drove past him.

A228

adj.—trite; without freshness or originality

Attending parties became **banal** after a few weeks.

Questions

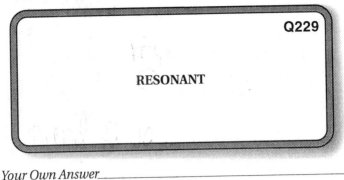

Q229

RESONANT

*Your Own Answer*_____

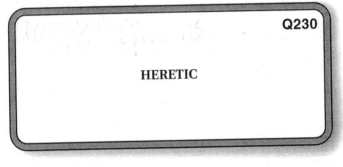

Q230

HERETIC

*Your Own Answer*_____

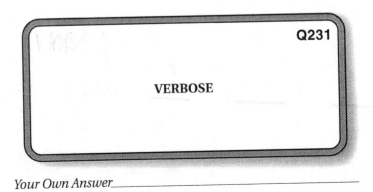

Q231

VERBOSE

*Your Own Answer*_____

Correct Answers

adj.—resounding; re-echoing
Beautiful **resonant** music escaped from the cathedral's windows.

n.—one who holds opinions contrary to that which is generally accepted

He was considered a **heretic** because he stopped believing in the strict doctrines of the religion he was brought up in.

adj.—wordy verbal communication
Because the boss is **verbose**, his meetings are usually lengthy.

Questions

Q232

NUGATORY

*Your Own Answer*_____

_____

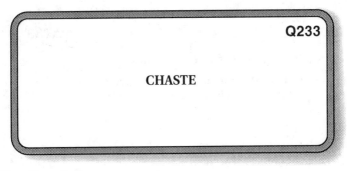

Q233

CHASTE

*Your Own Answer*_____

_____

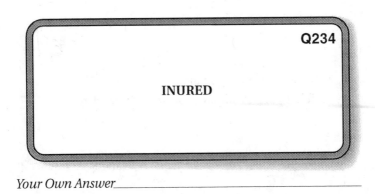

Q234

INURED

*Your Own Answer*_____

_____

Correct Answers

A232

adj.—trifling; futile; worthless; insignificant

Because the problem was **nugatory**, it was not addressed immediately.

A233

adj.—virtuous; free of obscenity

Because the woman believed in being **chaste**, she would not let her date into the house.

A234

adj.—accustomed to pain

Beekeepers eventually become **inured** to bee stings.

Questions

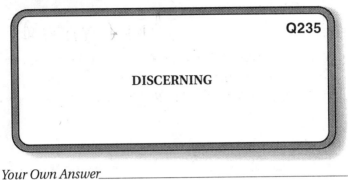

Q235

DISCERNING

*Your Own Answer*_____

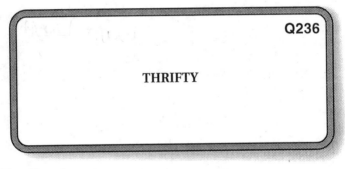

Q236

THRIFTY

*Your Own Answer*_____

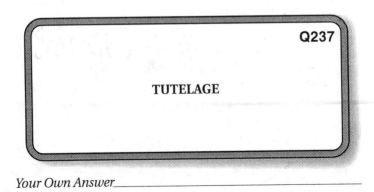

Q237

TUTELAGE

*Your Own Answer*_____

Correct Answers

A235

adj.—having good judgment

Being **discerning** about a customer's character is a key qualification for a loan officer.

A236

adj.—frugal; careful with money

Being **thrifty**, the woman would not purchase the item without a coupon.

A237

n.—the condition of being under a guardian or a tutor

Being under the **tutelage** of a master musician is a great honor.

Questions

EXPUNGE

*Your Own Answer*_____

BROACH

*Your Own Answer*_____

MYRIAD

*Your Own Answer*_____

Correct Answers

A238

v.—to blot out; to delete

Bleach may be used to **expunge** the stain.

A239

v.—to introduce into conversation

The supervisor found it difficult to **broach** the topic of the employee's poor work habits.

A240

n.—a large number

Buying an old house often necessitates fixing a **myriad** of problems.

Questions

Q241

FALLIBLE

*Your Own Answer*_____

Q242

CODA

*Your Own Answer*_____

Q243

SEETHE

*Your Own Answer*_____

Correct Answers

adj.—liable to be mistaken or erroneous

After being proven a **fallible** source several times, I decided to discard the reference book.

n.—in music, a concluding passage

By the end of the **coda**, I was ready to burst with excitement over the thrilling performance.

v.—to be violently disturbed

By the time I arrived, she was **seething** with anger.

Questions

GUILE

*Your Own Answer*_____

GAFFE

*Your Own Answer*_____

SUPPLANT

*Your Own Answer*_____

Correct Answers

n.—slyness in dealing with others

By using his **guile**, the gambler almost always won at the card table.

n.—a blunder

Calling the woman by the wrong name was a huge **gaffe**.

v.—to take the place of

Can you **supplant** my position if I cannot play?

Questions

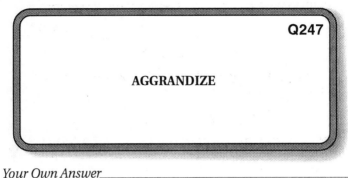

Q247

AGGRANDIZE

*Your Own Answer*_____

_____

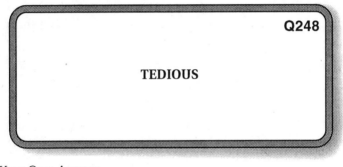

Q248

TEDIOUS

*Your Own Answer*_____

_____

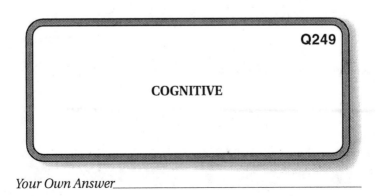

Q249

COGNITIVE

*Your Own Answer*_____

_____

Correct Answers

A247

v.—to make more powerful

Charlemagne sought to **aggrandize** himself and his kingdom.

A248

adj.—wearisome; tiresome

Cleaning the house is a **tedious** chore for some people.

A249

adj.—possessing the power to think or meditate; meditative; capable of perception

Cognitive thought makes humans adaptable to a quickly changing environment.

Questions

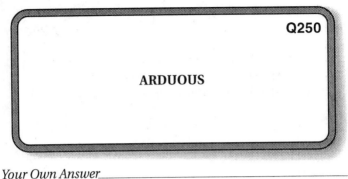

Q250

ARDUOUS

*Your Own Answer*_____

Q251

COMPLIANT

*Your Own Answer*_____

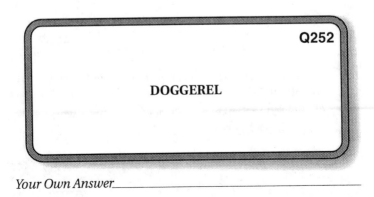

Q252

DOGGEREL

*Your Own Answer*_____

Correct Answers

A250

adj.—laborious; difficult; strenuous

Completing the plans for the school's expansion proved to be an **arduous** affair.

A251

adj.—complying; obeying; yielding

Compliant actions should be reinforced.

A252

n.—trivial, inartistic, weakly constructed verse, usually of a comic nature

Compared to Shakespeare's poetry, my best work reads like **doggerel**.

Questions

Q253

CRAVEN

*Your Own Answer*_____

Q254

TRANSMUTE

*Your Own Answer*_____

Q255

TERRESTRIAL

*Your Own Answer*_____

Correct Answers

A253

adj.—cowardly

Craven men will not stand up for what they believe in.

A254

v.—to transform

Decorators **transmute** ordinary homes into interesting showcases.

A255

adj.—pertaining to the earth

Deer are **terrestrial** animals; fish are aquatic.

Questions

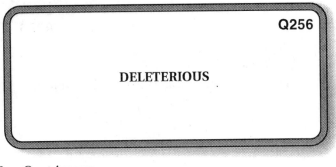

Q256

DELETERIOUS .

*Your Own Answer*_____

_____

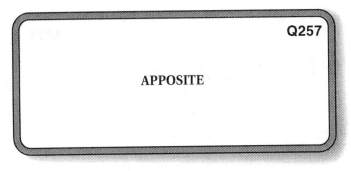

Q257

APPOSITE

*Your Own Answer*_____

_____

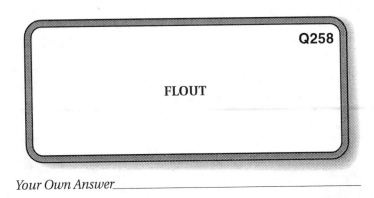

Q258

FLOUT

*Your Own Answer*_____

_____

Correct Answers

A256

adj.—harmful; hurtful; noxious
Deleterious fumes escaped from the overturned truck.

A257

adj.—suitable; apt; relevant
Discussion of poverty was **apposite** to the curriculum, so the professor allowed it.

A258

v.—to mock or jeer
Do not **flout** an opponent if you believe in fair play.

Questions

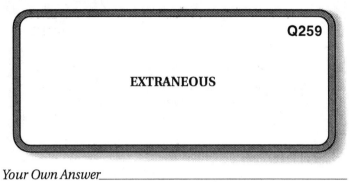

Q259

EXTRANEOUS

*Your Own Answer*_____

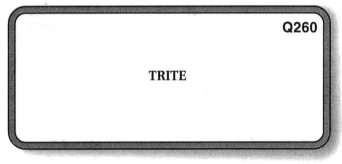

Q260

TRITE

*Your Own Answer*_____

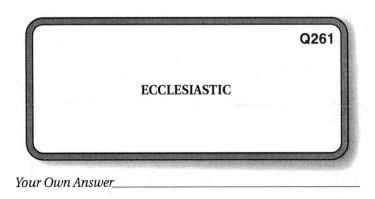

Q261

ECCLESIASTIC

*Your Own Answer*_____

Correct Answers

A259

adj.—irrelevant; not related; not essential
During the long, boring lecture, most people agreed
that much of the information was **extraneous**.

A260

adj.—becoming unoriginal through too much use
Eating tomato salads became **trite** after their excessive popularity.

A261

adj.—pertaining or relating to a church
Ecclesiastic obligations include attending mass.

Questions

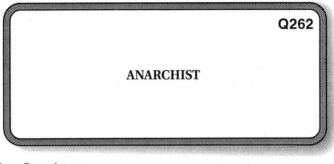

Q262

ANARCHIST

*Your Own Answer*_____

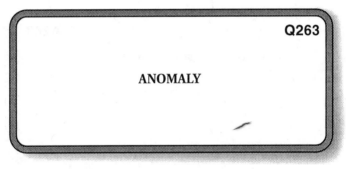

Q263

ANOMALY

*Your Own Answer*_____

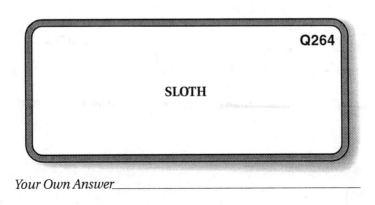

Q264

SLOTH

*Your Own Answer*_____

Correct Answers

n.—one who believes that a formal government is unnecessary

Eight **anarchists** were found guilty in the Haymarket riot.

n.—an oddity; an inconsistency; a deviation from the norm

El Niño has been known to create **anomalies** in the weather.

n.—aversion to work or exertion; laziness; sluggishness

The girl was fired because she was **slothful**.

Questions

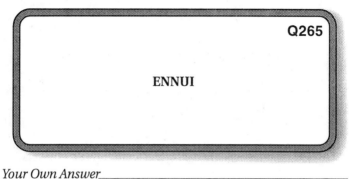

Q265

ENNUI

*Your Own Answer*_____

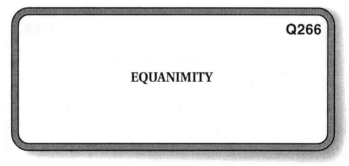

Q266

EQUANIMITY

*Your Own Answer*_____

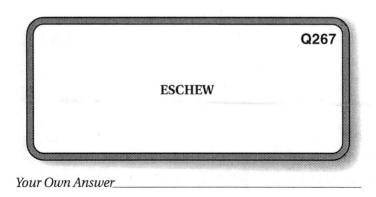

Q267

ESCHEW

*Your Own Answer*_____

Correct Answers

A265

n.—boredom; apathy

Ennui set in when the children realized they had already played with all the toys.

A266

n.—the quality of remaining calm and undisturbed

His ability for **equanimity** was not hampered, even by the car accident.

A267

v.—to shun; to avoid

Eschew the traffic and you may arrive on time.

Questions

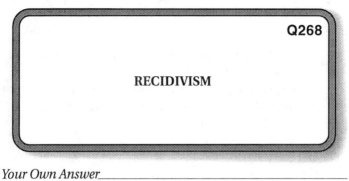

Q268

RECIDIVISM

*Your Own Answer*_____

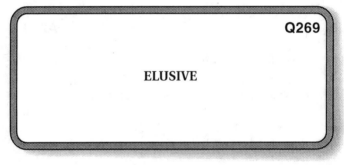

Q269

ELUSIVE

*Your Own Answer*_____

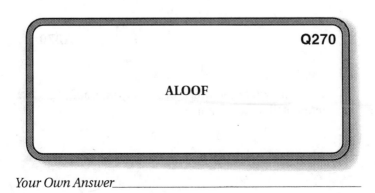

Q270

ALOOF

*Your Own Answer*_____

Correct Answers

A268

n.—habitual or chronic relapse of criminal or antisocial offenses

Even after intense therapy, the parolee experienced several episodes of **recidivism** and was eventually sent back to prison.

A269

adj.—hard to catch

Even the experienced, old fisherman admitted that the trout in the river were quite **elusive**.

A270

adj.—distant in interest; reserved; cool

Even though the new coworker stayed **aloof**, we attempted to be friendly.

Questions

Q271

QUIESCENT

*Your Own Answer*_____

_____

Q272

PRECLUDE

*Your Own Answer*_____

_____

Q273

EXULTATION

*Your Own Answer*_____

_____

Correct Answers

A271

adj.—inactive; quiet; at rest
Everyone deserves a day off and should remain **quiescent** on Sundays.

A272

v.—to prevent
Exercise may help to **preclude** heart disease.

A273

n.—the act of rejoicing
Exultation was evident by the partying and revelry.

Questions

Q274

FORTUITOUS

*Your Own Answer*_____

_____

Q275

REPREHEND

*Your Own Answer*_____

_____

Q276

DEIGN

*Your Own Answer*_____

_____

Correct Answers

adj.—happening accidentally
Finding the money under the bush was **fortuitous**.

v.—to reprimand; to find fault with
Finding the need to **reprehend** the student's actions, she gave her detention.

v.—to lower one's self in order to do something believed to be beneath one's dignity
Fired from his job as a programmer analyst, Joe vowed he would never **deign** to mop floors—even if he were down to his last penny.

Questions

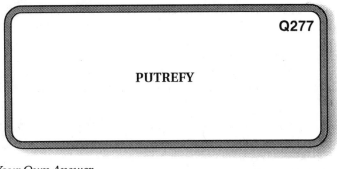

Q277

PUTREFY

*Your Own Answer*_____

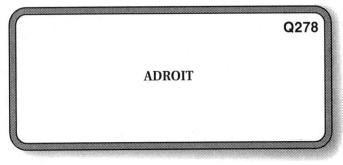

Q278

ADROIT

*Your Own Answer*_____

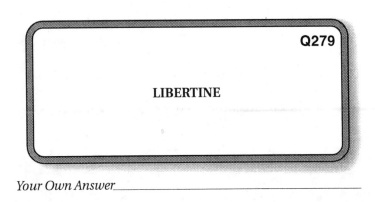

Q279

LIBERTINE

*Your Own Answer*_____

Correct Answers

A277

v.—to decompose; to rot
Food will begin to **putrefy** if exposed to air for too long.

A278

adj.—expert or skillful
For an **adroit** mechanic, the repair would be nothing.

A279

n.—one who indulges his desires without moral restraint
A man who frequently commits adultery may be considered a **libertine**.

Questions

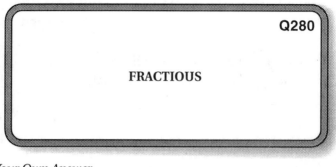

Q280

FRACTIOUS

*Your Own Answer*_____

Q281

HUMILITY

*Your Own Answer*_____

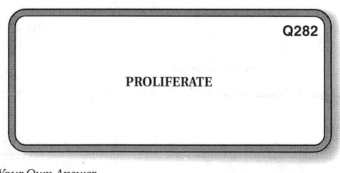

Q282

PROLIFERATE

*Your Own Answer*_____

Correct Answers

A280

adj.—rebellious; apt to quarrel; unruly
Fractious siblings aggravate their parents.

A281

n.—lack of pride; modesty
Full of **humility**, she accepted the award, but gave all the credit to her mentor.

A282

v.—to reproduce quickly
Gerbils are known to **proliferate**.

Questions

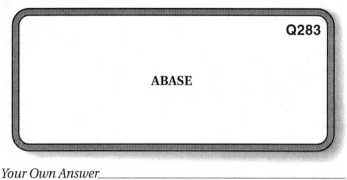

Q283

ABASE

*Your Own Answer*_____

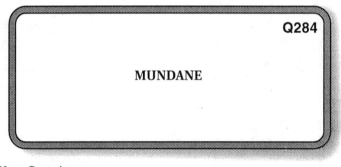

Q284

MUNDANE

*Your Own Answer*_____

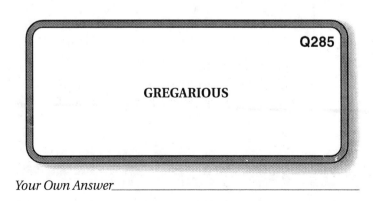

Q285

GREGARIOUS

*Your Own Answer*_____

Correct Answers

A283

v.—to degrade; to humiliate; to disgrace

Getting in-school detention was a sure way to **abase** the girl, the psychologist said.

A284

adj.—ordinary

Going food shopping soon became **mundane**, losing all of its excitement.

A285

adj.—fond of the company of others

Gregarious people may find those jobs with human contact more enjoyable than jobs that isolate them from the public.

Questions

Q286

SARDONIC

*Your Own Answer*_____

Q287

EMANATE

*Your Own Answer*_____

Q288

ASSAY

*Your Own Answer*_____

Correct Answers

A286

adj.—having a sarcastic quality
H.L. Mencken was known for his **sardonic** writings on political figures.

A287

v.—to emit
Happiness **emanates** from the loving home.

A288

v.—to determine the quality of a substance
The farmer **assayed** the soil to determine if it was good for growing crops.

Questions

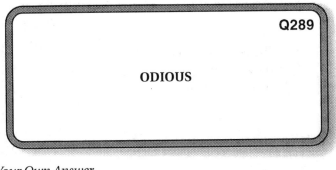

Q289

ODIOUS

*Your Own Answer*_____

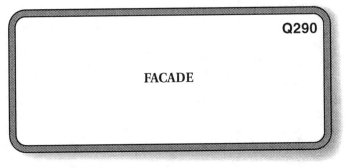

Q290

FACADE

*Your Own Answer*_____

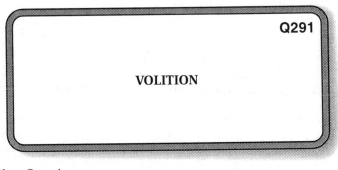

Q291

VOLITION

*Your Own Answer*_____

Correct Answers

A289

adj.—hateful; disgusting
Having to chaperone her brother was an **odious** chore for the girl.

A290

n.—front view; false appearance
He acted as though he was not bothered by her rejection, but it was all a **facade**.

A291

n.—the act of willing
He attended the meeting of his own **volition**.

Questions

VICISSITUDE

*Your Own Answer*_____

FORBEARANCE

*Your Own Answer*_____

VINDICATE

*Your Own Answer*_____

Correct Answers

A292

n.—unpredictable change occurring in life

He attributed his rise to fortune and fall into bankruptcy to the **vicissitudes** of life.

A293

n.—patience; self-restraint

He exhibited remarkable **forbearance** when confronted with the mischievous children.

A294

v.—to clear or defend against criticism or blame

He hired a lawyer to help **vindicate** him in court.

Questions

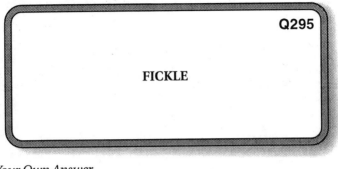

Q295

FICKLE

*Your Own Answer*_____

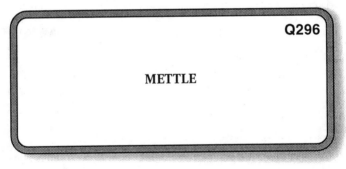

Q296

METTLE

*Your Own Answer*_____

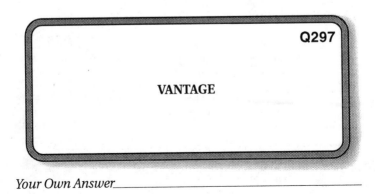

Q297

VANTAGE

*Your Own Answer*_____

Correct Answers

A295

adj.—changeable; unpredictable

He is quite **fickle**; just because he wants something today does not mean he will want it tomorrow.

A296

n.—spirit; courage; ardor

He proved he had the **mettle** to make it through basic training.

A297

n.—favorable position; position allowing a clear view or understanding

He was at a **vantage** point in his career and expected to be promoted soon.

Questions

Q298

BUMPTIOUS

*Your Own Answer*_____

_____

Q299

HAPHAZARD

*Your Own Answer*_____

_____

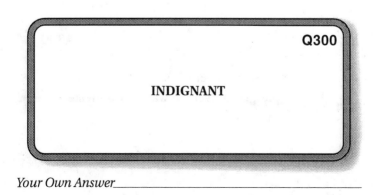

Q300

INDIGNANT

*Your Own Answer*_____

_____

Correct Answers

A298

adj.—arrogant

He was **bumptious** in manner as he approached the podium to accept his anticipated award.

A299

adj.—unplanned

He was constantly misplacing important documents; you could say he had a **haphazard** way of running his office.

A300

adj.—expressing anger to an injustice

He was **indignant** over the way he was treated.

Questions

Q301

QUIXOTIC

*Your Own Answer*_____

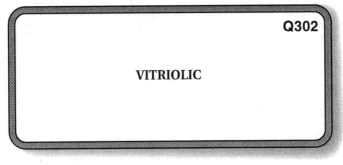

Q302

VITRIOLIC

*Your Own Answer*_____

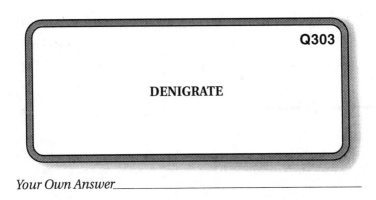

Q303

DENIGRATE

*Your Own Answer*_____

Correct Answers

A301

adj.—romantically idealistic; extravagantly chivalrous

He was popular with the ladies due to his **quixotic** charm.

A302

adj.—bitter

He was **vitriolic** after the confrontation.

A303

v.—to defame; to blacken or sully; to belittle

Her attempt to **denigrate** the man's name was not successful.

Questions

Q304

COPIOUS

*Your Own Answer*_____

Q305

GERMANE

*Your Own Answer*_____

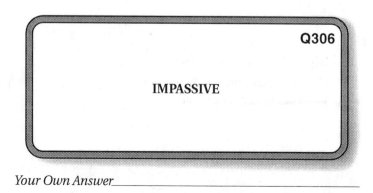

Q306

IMPASSIVE

*Your Own Answer*_____

Correct Answers

A304

adj.—abundant; in great quantities

Her **copious** notes touched on every subject presented in the lecture.

A305

adj.—relevant to the point

Her essay lacked enough **germane** information to warrant a failing grade.

A306

adj.—showing no emotion

Her expected announcement was met by an **impassive** facial expression.

Questions

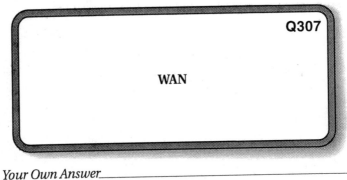

Q307

WAN

*Your Own Answer*_____

_____

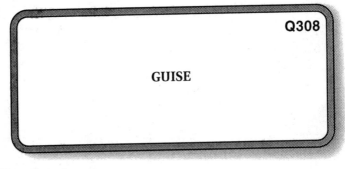

Q308

GUISE

*Your Own Answer*_____

_____

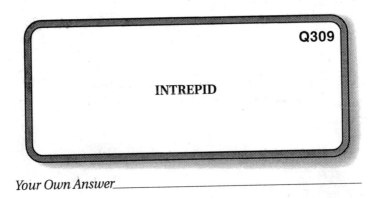

Q309

INTREPID

*Your Own Answer*_____

_____

Correct Answers

A307

adj.—lacking color; sickly pale
Her face became **wan** at the sight of blood.

A308

n.—appearance
Her **guise** was one of pure beauty.

A309

adj.—fearless; bold
Her **intrepid** actions deserved a medal.

Questions

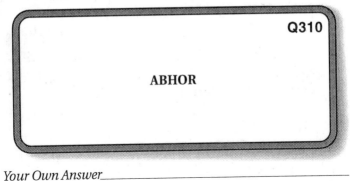

Q310

ABHOR

*Your Own Answer*_____

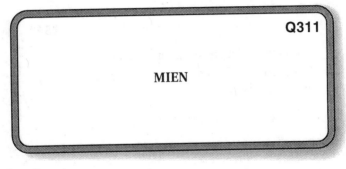

Q311

MIEN

*Your Own Answer*_____

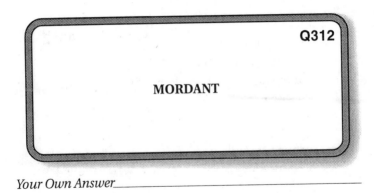

Q312

MORDANT

*Your Own Answer*_____

Correct Answers

A310

v.—to hate

Her jaw tensed at the sight of him; it wasn't hard to believe she **abhorred** the man.

A311

n.—appearance, bearing, or manner

Her **mien** was typically one of distress, especially after the mishap.

A312

adj.—cutting; sarcastic

Her **mordant** remark made me feel unqualified and useless.

Questions

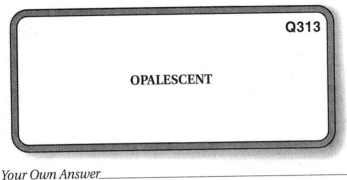

Q313

OPALESCENT

*Your Own Answer*_____

_____

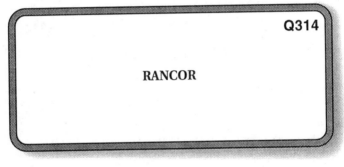

Q314

RANCOR

*Your Own Answer*_____

_____

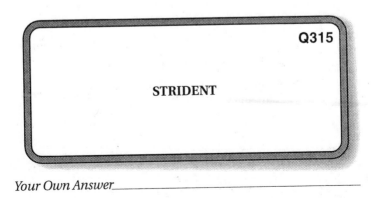

Q315

STRIDENT

*Your Own Answer*_____

_____

Correct Answers

A313

adj.—iridescent

Her new nail polish was **opalescent**, making her fingertips look like pearls.

A314

n.—strong ill will; enmity

Her **rancor** for the man was evident in her hateful expression.

A315

adj.—creaking; harsh; grating

Her **strident** voice hampered her chances of getting the announcer position.

Questions

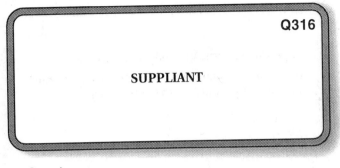

Q316

SUPPLIANT

*Your Own Answer*_____

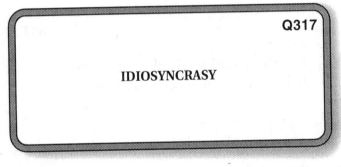

Q317

IDIOSYNCRASY

*Your Own Answer*_____

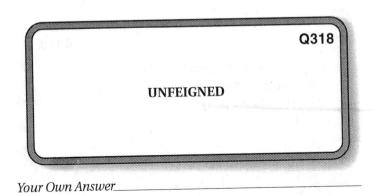

Q318

UNFEIGNED

*Your Own Answer*_____

Correct Answers

A316

adj.—asking earnestly and submissively
When she was called on, she asked in a **suppliant**
manner if she could go to the bathroom.

A317

n.—any personal peculiarity; mannerism
Her tendency to bite her lip is an **idiosyncrasy**.

A318

adj.—genuine; real; sincere
Her **unfeigned** reaction of surprise meant she had
not expected the party.

Questions

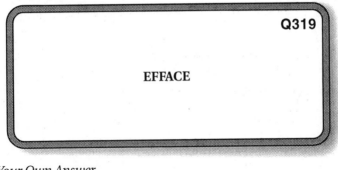

Q319

EFFACE

*Your Own Answer*_____

_____

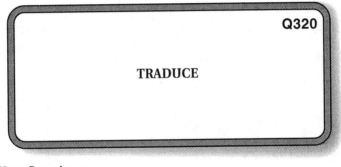

Q320

TRADUCE

*Your Own Answer*_____

_____

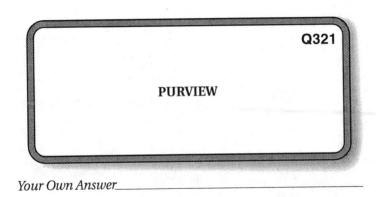

Q321

PURVIEW

*Your Own Answer*_____

_____

Correct Answers

A319

v.—to erase; to make inconspicuous
Hiding in the woods, the soldier was **effaced** by his camouflage uniform.

A320

v.—to defame or slander
His actions **traduced** his reputation.

A321

n.—the extent of something
His actions were within the **purview** of the law.

Questions

Q322

FESTER

*Your Own Answer*_____

Q323

HINDRANCE

*Your Own Answer*_____

Q324

BLASPHEMOUS

*Your Own Answer*_____

Correct Answers

A322

v.—to become more and more virulent and fixed
His anger **festered** until no one could change his mind.

A323

n.—blockage; obstacle
His assistance often seems to be more of a **hindrance** than a help.

A324

adj.—speaking ill of; using profane language
His **blasphemous** outburst was heard throughout the room, and offended everyone in it.

Questions

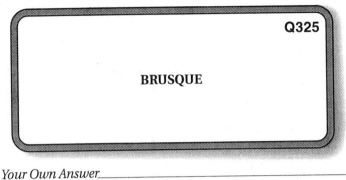

Q325

BRUSQUE

*Your Own Answer*_____

_____

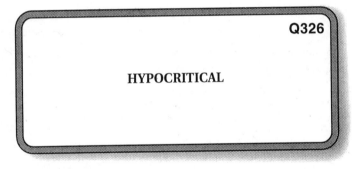

Q326

HYPOCRITICAL

*Your Own Answer*_____

_____

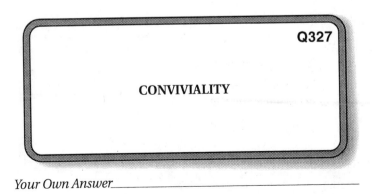

Q327

CONVIVIALITY

*Your Own Answer*_____

_____

Correct Answers

adj.—abrupt in manner or speech; discourteously blunt

His **brusque** answer was unacceptable.

adj.—two-faced; deceptive

His constituents believed that the governor was **hypocritical** for calling for a moratorium on "negative" campaigning while continuing to air some of the most vicious ads ever produced against his opponent.

n.—a fondness for festiveness or joviality

His **conviviality** makes him a welcome guest at any social gathering.

Questions

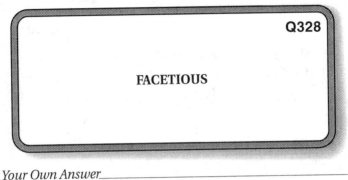

Q328

FACETIOUS

*Your Own Answer*_____

_____

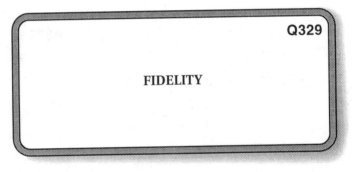

Q329

FIDELITY

*Your Own Answer*_____

_____

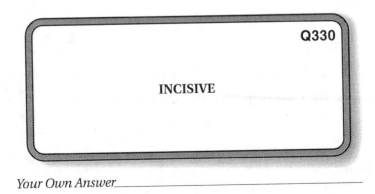

Q330

INCISIVE

*Your Own Answer*_____

_____

Correct Answers

A328

adj.—joking in an awkward or improper manner
His **facetious** sarcasm was inappropriate during his first staff meeting.

A329

n.—faithfulness; honesty
His **fidelity** was proven when he turned in the lost money.

A330

adj.—getting to the heart of things; to the point
His **incisive** questioning helped settle the matter quickly.

Questions

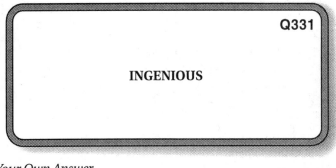

Q331

INGENIOUS

*Your Own Answer*_____

Q332

SLOVENLY

*Your Own Answer*_____

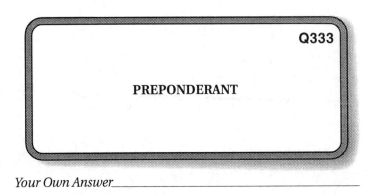

Q333

PREPONDERANT

*Your Own Answer*_____

Correct Answers

A331

adj.—clever; resourceful

His **ingenious** idea made it possible to double production at no extra cost.

A332

adv.—sloppy

His mother-in-law did not approve of his **slovenly** manner.

A333

adj.—to outweigh; to be superior in amount, weight, etc.

His positive qualities are **preponderant** over his occasional rudeness.

Questions

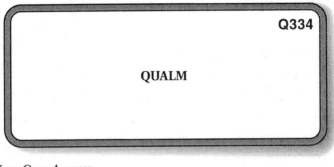

Q334

QUALM

*Your Own Answer*_____

_____

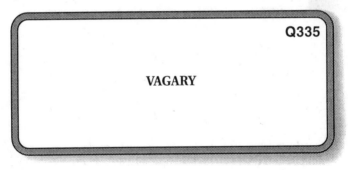

Q335

VAGARY

*Your Own Answer*_____

_____

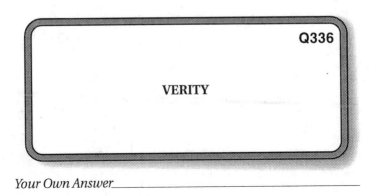

Q336

VERITY

*Your Own Answer*_____

_____

Correct Answers

A334

n.—sudden feeling of uneasiness or doubt

His **qualms** about flying disappeared once the plane took off.

A335

n.—an odd or eccentric action

His talking to trees was a **vagary** to his puzzled neighbors.

A336

n.—truth

His testimony was given with **verity**.

Questions

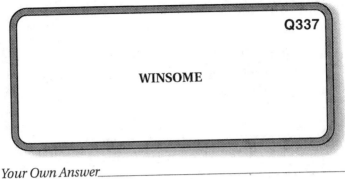

Q337

WINSOME

*Your Own Answer*_____

_____

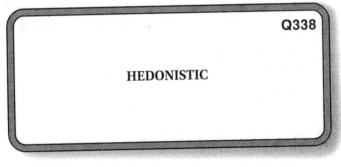

Q338

HEDONISTIC

*Your Own Answer*_____

_____

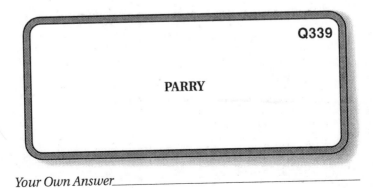

Q339

PARRY

*Your Own Answer*_____

_____

Correct Answers

A337

adj.—charming; sweetly attractive

His **winsome** words moved the crowd to love him even more.

A338

adj.—pleasure seeking

Hot tubs, good food, and a plethora of leisure time are hallmarks of this **hedonistic** society.

A339

v.—to avoid; to ward off

I dislike talking to the woman so I will attempt to **parry** her by ducking around the corner.

Questions

Q340

VERBIAGE

*Your Own Answer*_____

Q341

CALUMNY

*Your Own Answer*_____

Q342

PENCHANT

*Your Own Answer*_____

Correct Answers

A340

n.—wordiness
I enjoy speeches that contain little **verbiage**.

A341

n.—slander
I felt it necessary to speak against the **calumny** of the man's good reputation.

A342

n.—a strong liking
I have a **penchant** for ice cream.

Questions

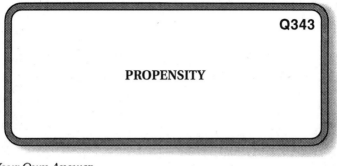

Q343

PROPENSITY

*Your Own Answer*_____

Q344

CONUNDRUM

*Your Own Answer*_____

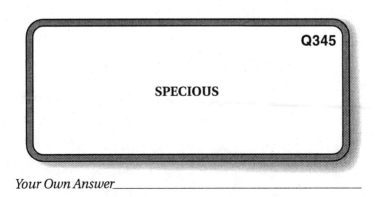

Q345

SPECIOUS

*Your Own Answer*_____

Correct Answers

n.—an inclination; a natural tendency toward
I have a strong **propensity** for writing, and I like to read as well.

n.—a puzzle or riddle
I spent two hours trying to figure out the **conundrum**.

adj.—plausible, apparently good or right though lacking real merit
The politician lost the election because the voters could see right through his **specious** arguments.

Questions

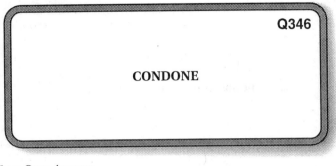

Q346

CONDONE

*Your Own Answer*_____

_____

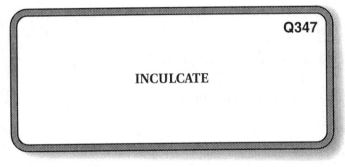

Q347

INCULCATE

*Your Own Answer*_____

_____

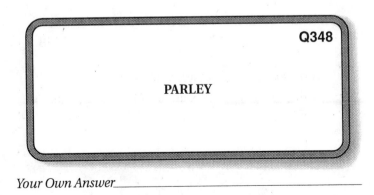

Q348

PARLEY

*Your Own Answer*_____

_____

Correct Answers

A346

v.—to forgive
I will **condone** your actions of negligence.

A347

v.—to impress upon the mind by persistent urging
Her religious beliefs were **inculcated** at a young age by her grandparents.

A348

v.—to speak with another; to discourse
I will **parley** the information to the appropriate person.

Questions

Q349

IMPUGN

*Your Own Answer*_____

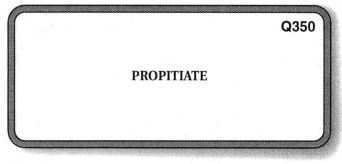

Q350

PROPITIATE

*Your Own Answer*_____

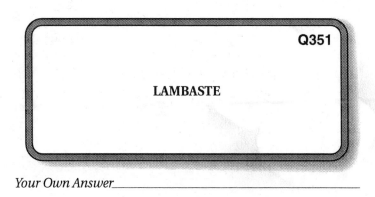

Q351

LAMBASTE

*Your Own Answer*_____

Correct Answers

A349

v.—to attack verbally; to criticize; to refute

If I believe the man is a fraud, I will **impugn** his comments.

A350

v.—to win the goodwill of

If I try my best, I will hopefully **propitiate** my new supervisor.

A351

v.—to beat harshly or scold

If the boy breaks the lamp, his father will surely **lambaste** him.

Questions

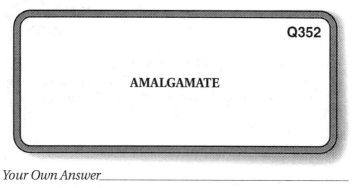

Q352

AMALGAMATE

*Your Own Answer*_____

Q353

HEED

*Your Own Answer*_____

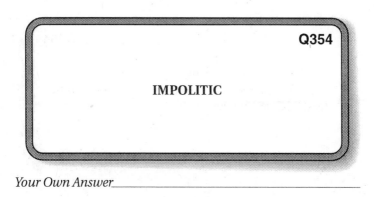

Q354

IMPOLITIC

*Your Own Answer*_____

Correct Answers

A352

v.—to mix; to merge; to combine

If the economy does not grow, the apparel maker may need to **amalgamate** with a rival company.

A353

v.—to obey; to yield to

If the peasant **heeds** the king's commands, she will be able to keep her land.

A354

adj.—unwise; imprudent

If you are planning to invest your money, **impolitic** decisions may be costly.

Questions

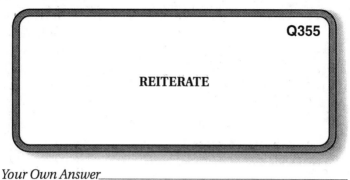

Q355

REITERATE

*Your Own Answer*_____

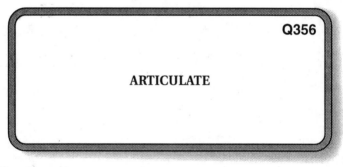

Q356

ARTICULATE

*Your Own Answer*_____

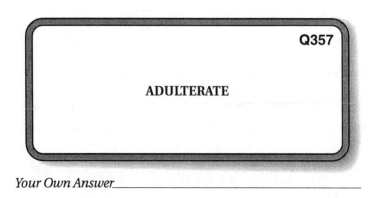

Q357

ADULTERATE

*Your Own Answer*_____

Correct Answers

v.—to say again

If you did not hear me the first time, I will **reiterate** the directions for you.

adj.—clear; distinct; expressed with clarity; skillful with words

If you want to get your point across, it helps to be **articulate**.

v.—to corrupt, debase, or make impure

Illegal dumping has **adulterated** the lake.

Questions

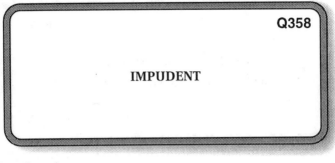

Q358

IMPUDENT

*Your Own Answer*_____

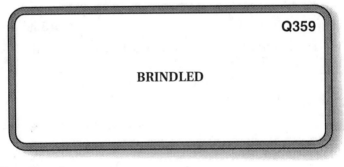

Q359

BRINDLED

*Your Own Answer*_____

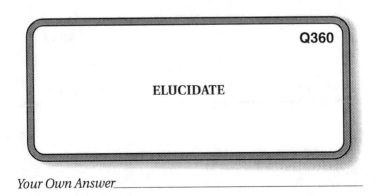

Q360

ELUCIDATE

*Your Own Answer*_____

Correct Answers

A358

adj.—disrespectful; shameless; rude
Impudent actions caused him to be unpopular.

A359

adj.—streaked or spotted with a darker color; said especially of animals' coats
The puppy's **brindled** coat made him stand out from the rest of the litter.

A360

v.—to make clear; to explain
In the paper's conclusion, its purpose was **elucidated** in one sentence.

Questions

BEHOOVE

*Your Own Answer*_____

_____

LITHE

*Your Own Answer*_____

_____

DERIDE

*Your Own Answer*_____

_____

Correct Answers

A361

v.—to be necessary; to be incumbent upon
It **behooves** the student to study for the test.

A362

adj.—easily bent; pliable; supple
It is best to use a **lithe** material when constructing a curved object.

A363

v.—to laugh at with contempt; to mock
It is impolite to **deride** someone even if you dislike him.

Questions

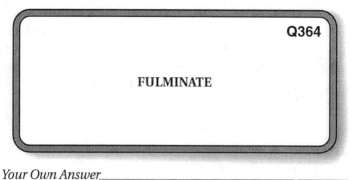

Q364

FULMINATE

*Your Own Answer*_____

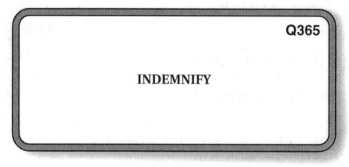

Q365

INDEMNIFY

*Your Own Answer*_____

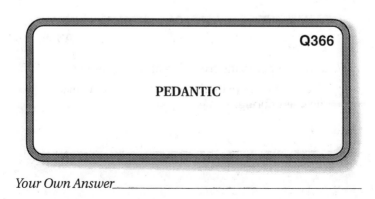

Q366

PEDANTIC

*Your Own Answer*_____

Correct Answers

A364

v.—to issue denunciations; to condemn

The teacher **fulminated** against the proposal for shorter class periods.

A365

v.—to insure against or pay for loss or damage

It is important to **indemnify** your valuables with a reliable insurance company.

A366

adj.—emphasizing trivial points of learning

The professor's **pedantic** manner of teaching made the class boring.

Questions

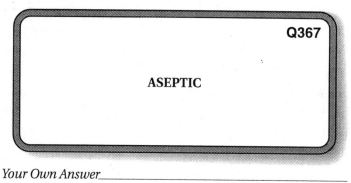

Q367

ASEPTIC

*Your Own Answer*_____

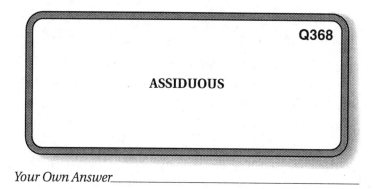

Q368

ASSIDUOUS

*Your Own Answer*_____

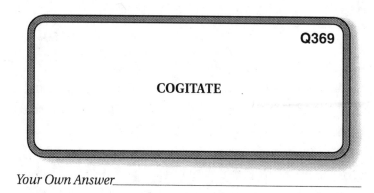

Q369

COGITATE

*Your Own Answer*_____

Correct Answers

A367

adj.—germ free
It is necessary for an operating room to be **aseptic**.

A368

adj.—carefully attentive; industrious
It is necessary to be **assiduous** if a person wishes to make the most of his time at work.

A369

v.—to think hard; ponder; meditate
It is necessary to **cogitate** on decisions which affect life goals.

Questions

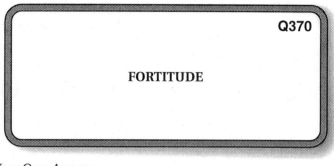

Q370

FORTITUDE

*Your Own Answer*_____

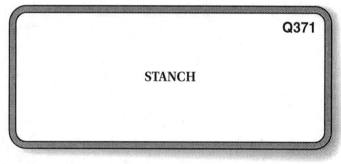

Q371

STANCH

*Your Own Answer*_____

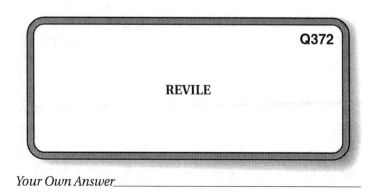

Q372

REVILE

*Your Own Answer*_____

Correct Answers

A370

n.—firm courage; strength

It is necessary to have **fortitude** to complete the hike.

A371

v.—to stop or check the flow of; to staunch

It is necessary to **stanch** the bleeding from the wound as soon as possible.

A372

v.—to be abusive in speech

It is not appropriate for a teacher to **revile** a student.

Questions

Q373

FEIGN

*Your Own Answer*_____

Q374

PRATE

*Your Own Answer*_____

Q375

PURLOIN

*Your Own Answer*_____

Correct Answers

A373

v.—to pretend

It is not uncommon for a child to **feign** illness in order to stay home from school.

A374

v.—to talk foolishly; chatter

It is not uncommon for people to **prate** when they become nervous about speaking to a superior.

A375

v.—to steal

She was known to **purloin** magazines from the local newsstand.

Questions

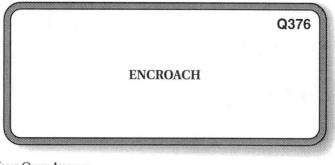

Q376

ENCROACH

*Your Own Answer*_____

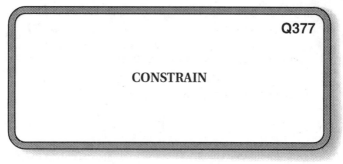

Q377

CONSTRAIN

*Your Own Answer*_____

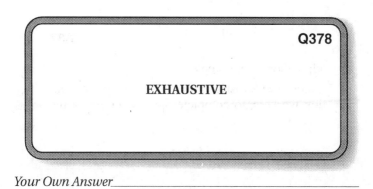

Q378

EXHAUSTIVE

*Your Own Answer*_____

Correct Answers

A376

v.—to trespass or intrude

It is unlawful to **encroach** on another's private property.

A377

v.—to force; to compel; to restrain

It may be necessary to **constrain** the wild animal if it approaches the town.

A378

adj.—thorough; complete

It took an **exhaustive** effort, using many construction workers, to complete the new home by the deadline.

Questions

Q379

FUTILE

*Your Own Answer*_____

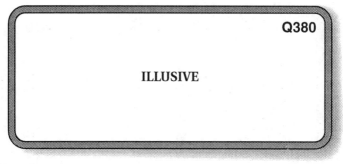

Q380

ILLUSIVE

*Your Own Answer*_____

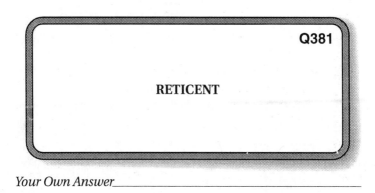

Q381

RETICENT

*Your Own Answer*_____

Correct Answers

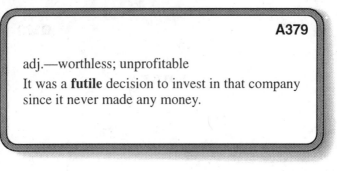

A379

adj.—worthless; unprofitable
It was a **futile** decision to invest in that company
since it never made any money.

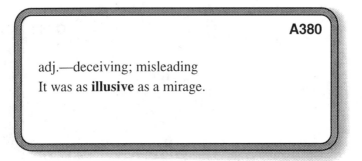

A380

adj.—deceiving; misleading
It was as **illusive** as a mirage.

A381

adj.—reserved; typically quiet
It was difficult to get the **reticent** boy to join the
conversation.

Questions

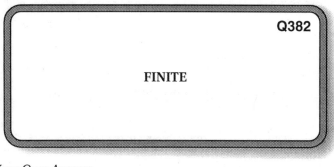

Q382

FINITE

*Your Own Answer*_____

_____

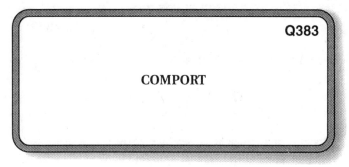

Q383

COMPORT

*Your Own Answer*_____

_____

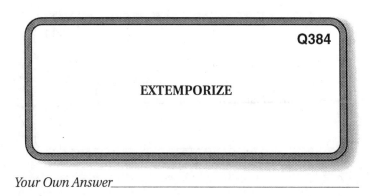

Q384

EXTEMPORIZE

*Your Own Answer*_____

_____

Correct Answers

A382

adj.—measurable; limited; not everlasting

It was discovered decades ago that the universe is not **finite**; it has unknown limits which cannot be measured.

A383

v.—to behave in a specified manner in order to fit in

Once he **comported** with his coworkers, he no longer felt like an outsider.

A384

v.—to improvise; to make it up as you go along

It was necessary for the musician to **extemporize** when his music fell off the stand.

Questions

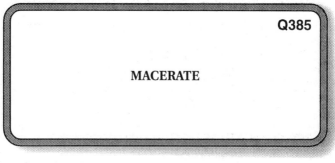

Q385

MACERATE

*Your Own Answer*_____

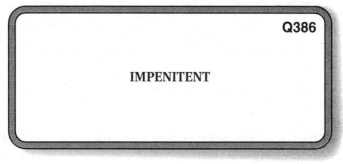

Q386

IMPENITENT

*Your Own Answer*_____

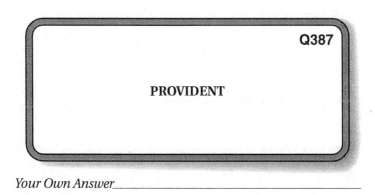

Q387

PROVIDENT

*Your Own Answer*_____

Correct Answers

A385

v.—to soften by steeping in liquid

It was necessary to **macerate** the food before the elderly man could eat it.

A386

adj.—without regret, shame, or remorse

It was obvious after his **impenitent** remark to the press that the defendant felt no remorse for his crime.

A387

adj.—prudent; economical; characterized by foresight

It was **provident**, in his opinion, to wait and buy the new car when he was financially secure.

Questions

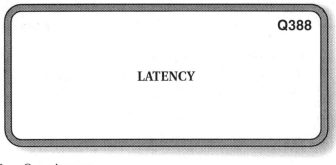

Q388

LATENCY

*Your Own Answer*_____

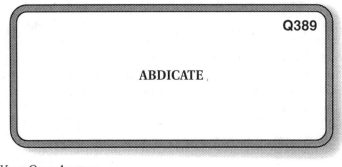

Q389

ABDICATE

*Your Own Answer*_____

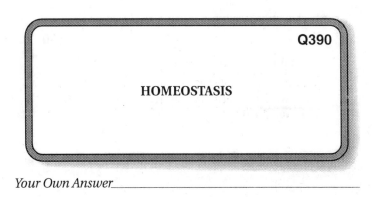

Q390

HOMEOSTASIS

*Your Own Answer*_____

Correct Answers

A388

n.—a period of inactivity

Its **latency** was small solace for the girl who feared that the cancer would re-emerge fiercer than ever.

A389

v.—to reject, renounce, or abandon

King Edward VIII sent shock waves through the U.K. by **abdicating** the throne to marry a commoner.

A390

n.—maintenance of stability

Knowing the seriousness of the operation, the surgeons were concerned about restoring the patient to **homeostasis.**

Questions

LASCIVIOUS

*Your Own Answer*_____

STYMIE

*Your Own Answer*_____

PSEUDONYM

*Your Own Answer*_____

Correct Answers

A391

adj.—characterized by lust

Known as a skirt chaser, his **lascivious** ways seemed to all but preclude a stable marriage.

A392

v.—to hinder or obstruct

Large amounts of snowfall will **stymie** the rescue effort.

A393

n.—a borrowed or fictitious name

Larry was a **pseudonym** for the reporter, who did not want to use his real name.

Questions

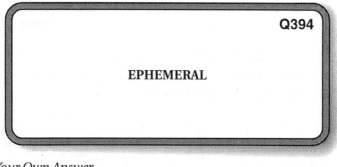

Q394

EPHEMERAL

*Your Own Answer*_____

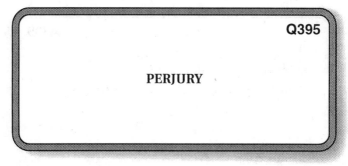

Q395

PERJURY

*Your Own Answer*_____

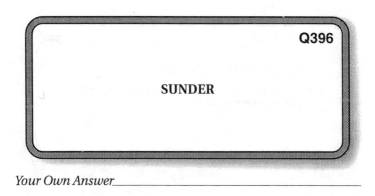

Q396

SUNDER

*Your Own Answer*_____

Correct Answers

A394

adj.—very short-lived; lasting only a short time

Living alone gave him **ephemeral** contentment, soon to be replaced by utter loneliness.

A395

n.—lying while under oath

Lying while on the witness stand is **perjury**.

A396

v.—to separate or break apart

Management seeks to **sunder** the workers' connections to the union.

Questions

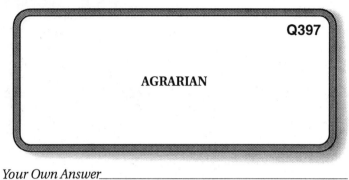

Q397

AGRARIAN

*Your Own Answer*_____

_____

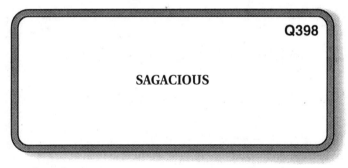

Q398

SAGACIOUS

*Your Own Answer*_____

_____

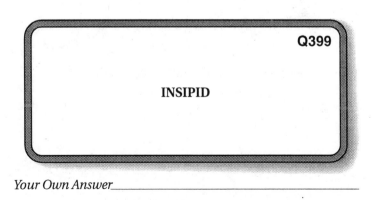

Q399

INSIPID

*Your Own Answer*_____

_____

Correct Answers

A397

adj.—of the land
Before the industrial revolution, most sectors of the country were **agrarian**.

A398

adj.—wise
Many of her friends came to her with their problems because she gave **sagacious** advice.

A399

adj.—uninteresting; boring; flat; dull
Many people left the **insipid** movie before it was finished.

Questions

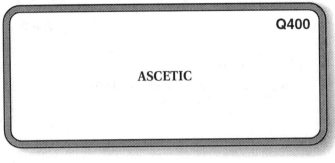

Q400

ASCETIC

*Your Own Answer*_____

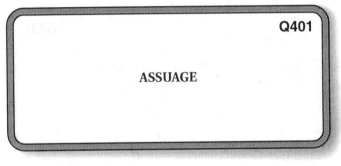

Q401

ASSUAGE

*Your Own Answer*_____

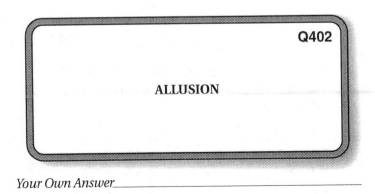

Q402

ALLUSION

*Your Own Answer*_____

Correct Answers

A400

adj.—self-denying
Many religious people lead **ascetic** lives.

A401

v.—to relieve; to ease; to make less severe
Medication should **assuage** the pain.

A402

n.—an indirect reference (often literary); a hint
Mention of the snake was an **allusion** to the man's
sneaky ways.

Questions

Q403

FOIBLE

*Your Own Answer*_____

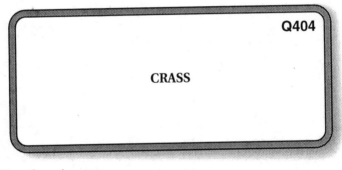

Q404

CRASS

*Your Own Answer*_____

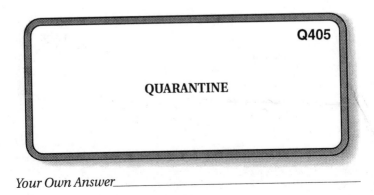

Q405

QUARANTINE

*Your Own Answer*_____

Correct Answers

A403

n.—a minor weakness of character
My major **foible** is an inability to resist chocolate.

A404

adj.—stupid; unrefined; gross
My respect for the man was lowered when he made the **crass** remark.

A405

n.—isolation of a person to prevent spread of disease
No one knew if the illness was contagious, so anyone who had the symptoms was put in **quarantine**.

Questions

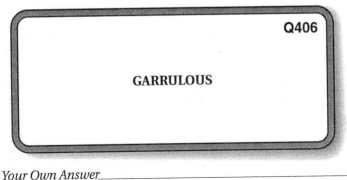

Q406

GARRULOUS

*Your Own Answer*_____

_____

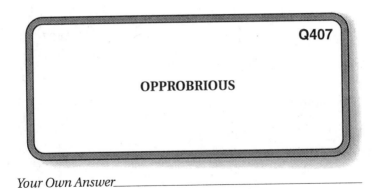

Q407

OPPROBRIOUS

*Your Own Answer*_____

_____

Q408

EQUINOX

*Your Own Answer*_____

_____

Correct Answers

A406

adj.—extremely talkative or wordy

No one wanted to speak with the **garrulous** man for fear of being stuck in a long, one-sided conversation.

A407

adj.—abusive

Nobody liked working for him because he was so **opprobrious**.

A408

n.—precise time when the day and night is of equal length

On the **equinox**, we had twelve hours of night and day.

Questions

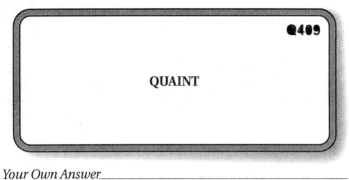

Q409

QUAINT

*Your Own Answer*_____

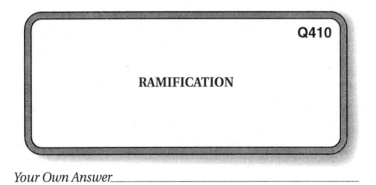

Q410

RAMIFICATION

*Your Own Answer*_____

Q411

PRIVY

*Your Own Answer*_____

Correct Answers

A409

adj.—old-fashioned; unusual; odd
One of the best qualities of the bed-and-breakfast was its **quaint** setting in the charming English village.

A410

n.—consequence
One of the **ramifications** of driving fast may be getting a speeding ticket.

A411

adj—to know secret knowledge
Only the woman's best friend was **privy** to her secret.

Questions

Q412

DEBONAIR

*Your Own Answer*_____

_____

Q413

RACONTEUR

*Your Own Answer*_____

_____

Q414

KITH

*Your Own Answer*_____

_____

Correct Answers

A412

adj.—having an affable manner; carefree; genial
Opening the door for another is a **debonair** action.

A413

n.—a person skilled at telling stories
Our entertainment was a **raconteur** who told a story of talking animals.

A414

n.—relatives and acquaintances
Our **kith** and kin will meet at the family reunion.

Questions

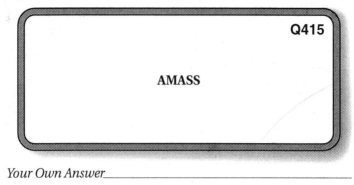

Q415

AMASS

*Your Own Answer*_____

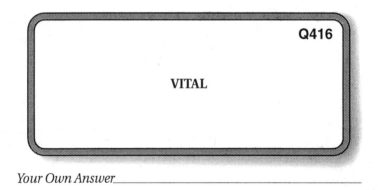

Q416

VITAL

*Your Own Answer*_____

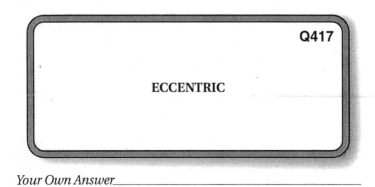

Q417

ECCENTRIC

*Your Own Answer*_____

Correct Answers

A415

v.—to collect together; to accumulate
Over the years the sailor has **amassed** many boat replicas.

A416

adj.—extremely important; crucial
Oxygen and food are **vital** for sustaining life.

A417

adj.—odd; peculiar; strange
People like to talk with the **eccentric** artist since he has such different views on everyday subjects.

Questions

Q418

DALLY

*Your Own Answer*_____

Q419

FRUGALITY

*Your Own Answer*_____

Q420

JUDICIOUS

*Your Own Answer*_____

Correct Answers

A418

v.—to loiter; to waste time

Please do not **dally** or we will miss our appointment.

A419

n.—thrift

Preparing to save money to send their daughter to college, the parents practiced extreme **frugality** for several years.

A420

adj.—using sound judgment

Putting money away for a rainy day is a **judicious** decision.

Questions

Q421

PROPAGATE

*Your Own Answer*_____

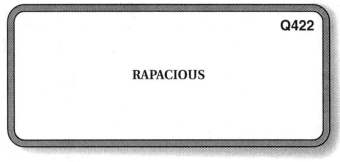

Q422

RAPACIOUS

*Your Own Answer*_____

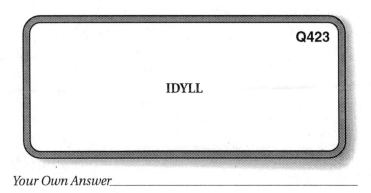

Q423

IDYLL

*Your Own Answer*_____

Correct Answers

v.—to reproduce or multiply
Rabbits and gerbils are said to **propagate** quickly.

adj.—given to seizing for plunder or the satisfaction of greed
The **rapacious** villain held the elderly lady hostage until the money was given to him.

n.—a written piece of work describing a peaceful rural scene
Reading the **idyll** made me think of the family farm.

Questions

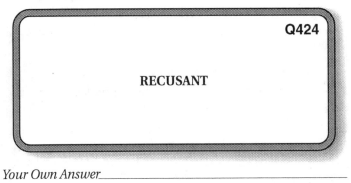

Q424

RECUSANT

*Your Own Answer*_____

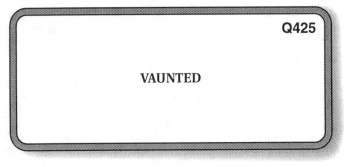

Q425

VAUNTED

*Your Own Answer*_____

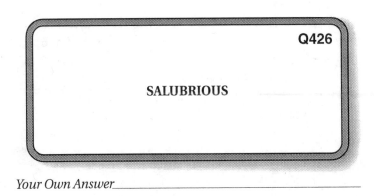

Q426

SALUBRIOUS

*Your Own Answer*_____

Correct Answers

A424

adj.—disobedient of authority
Recusant inmates may be denied privileges.

A425

adj.—boastful
The man showed us pictures of the **vaunted** gardens he visited in Holland.

A426

adj.—promoting good health
Eating well and exercising regularly are **salubrious** practices.

Questions

Q427

APOCALYPTIC

*Your Own Answer*_____

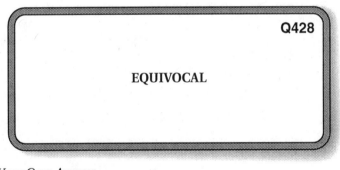

Q428

EQUIVOCAL

*Your Own Answer*_____

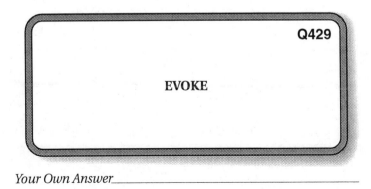

Q429

EVOKE

*Your Own Answer*_____

Correct Answers

adj.—predicting or presaging universal destruction

Science fiction movies seem to relish **apocalyptic** visions.

adj.—questionable; deliberately ambiguous

The criminal gave **equivocal** answers to the police officer's questions, so they brought him to the station for more interrogation.

v.—to call forth; to provoke

Seeing her only daughter get married **evoked** tears of happiness from the mother.

Questions

Q430

PEDAGOGUE

*Your Own Answer*_____

Q431

SERENDIPITY

*Your Own Answer*_____

Q432

COGNIZANT

*Your Own Answer*_____

Correct Answers

A430

n.—a teacher

Seeing the way she worked with children, there was no doubt she was a true **pedagogue**.

A431

n.—an apparent aptitude for making fortunate discoveries accidentally

It could only have been **serendipity** that brought him to his long-lost sister's house that rainy night.

A432

adj.—aware of

She was alarmed when she became **cognizant** of the man following her.

Questions

Q433

ARCANE

*Your Own Answer*_____

Q434

DISDAIN

*Your Own Answer*_____

Q435

EBULLIENCE

*Your Own Answer*_____

Correct Answers

A433

adj.—obscure; secret; mysterious

She commands broad knowledge of fire ants' mating habits and other **arcane** matters.

A434

v.—to reject with scorn

She **disdained** the man's advances.

A435

n.—an overflowing of high spirits; effervescence

She emanated **ebullience** as she skipped down the hallway and sang after learning of her promotion.

Questions

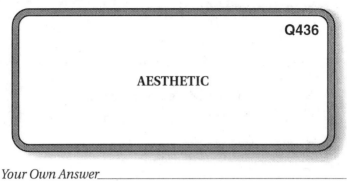

Q436

AESTHETIC

*Your Own Answer*_____

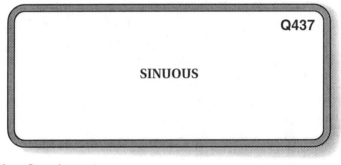

Q437

SINUOUS

*Your Own Answer*_____

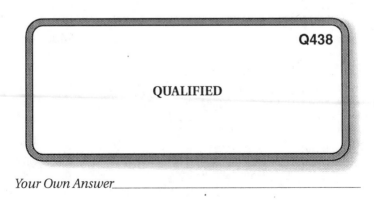

Q438

QUALIFIED

*Your Own Answer*_____

Correct Answers

A436

adj.—of beauty; pertaining to taste in art and beauty

She found her own **aesthetic** sense and that of the artist to be at odds.

A437

adj.—full of curves; twisting and turning

She lost control of her car on the **sinuous** road.

A438

adj.—experienced

She was well **qualified** for the job after working in the field for ten years.

Questions

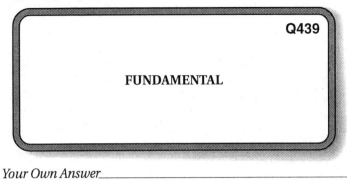

Q439

FUNDAMENTAL

*Your Own Answer*_____

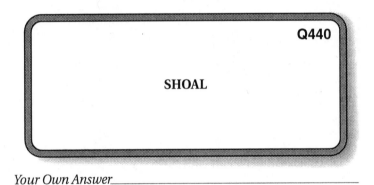

Q440

SHOAL

*Your Own Answer*_____

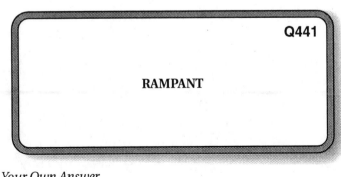

Q441

RAMPANT

*Your Own Answer*_____

Correct Answers

adj.—basic; necessary
Shelter is one of the **fundamental** needs of human existence.

n.—a large group or crowd
Shoals of tourists visit the Statue of Liberty each year.

adj.—growing unchecked; widespread
Social unrest was **rampant** because of the lack of food available to the people.

Questions

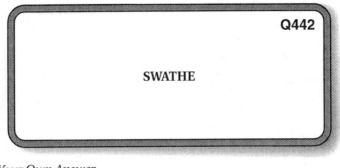

Q442

SWATHE

*Your Own Answer*_____

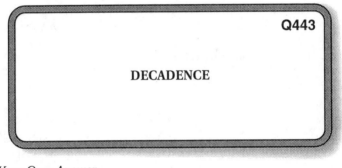

Q443

DECADENCE

*Your Own Answer*_____

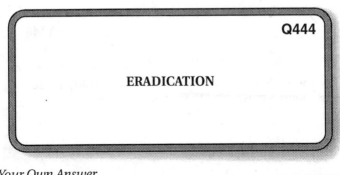

Q444

ERADICATION

*Your Own Answer*_____

Correct Answers

v.—to wrap around something; to envelop
Soft blankets **swathe** the newborn baby.

n.—a decline in morals or art
Some believe the **decadence** of Nero's rule led to
the fall of the empire.

n.—the act of annihilating, destroying, or erasing
Some have theorized that the **eradication** of the
dinosaurs was due to a radical change in climate.

Questions

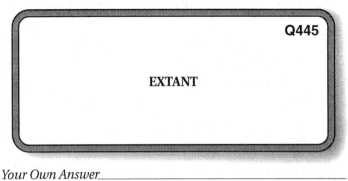

Q445

EXTANT

*Your Own Answer*_____

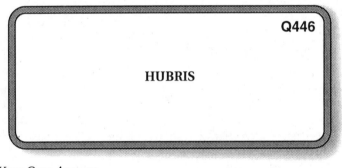

Q446

HUBRIS

*Your Own Answer*_____

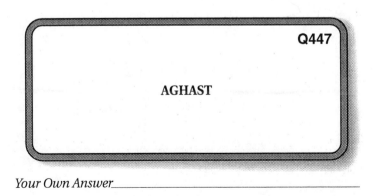

Q447

AGHAST

*Your Own Answer*_____

Correct Answers

A445

adj.—still existing; refers especially to books, documents, or species of animals

Some of my ancestors' letters remain **extant**.

A446

n.—arrogance

Some think it was **hubris** that brought the President to the point of impeachment.

A447

adj.—astonished; amazed; horrified; terrified; appalled

Stockholders were **aghast** at the company's revelation about unfair labor practices.

Questions

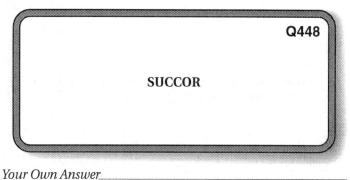

Q448

SUCCOR

*Your Own Answer*_____

_____

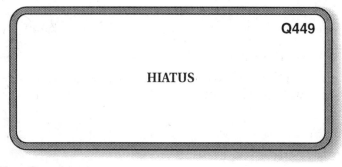

Q449

HIATUS

*Your Own Answer*_____

_____

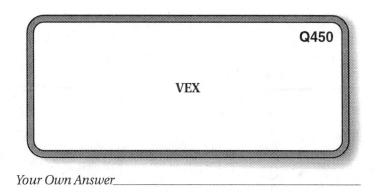

Q450

VEX

*Your Own Answer*_____

_____

Correct Answers

A448

n.—aid; assistance

Succor was given to the fire victim in the form of clothes and temporary shelter.

A449

n.—interval; break; period of rest

Summer vacation provided a much-needed **hiatus** for the students.

A450

v.—to be troublesome to; to annoy

Tardiness by employees may **vex** the superior.

Questions

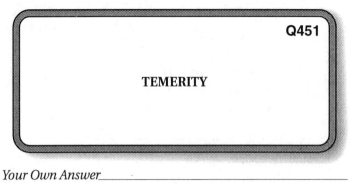

Q451

TEMERITY

*Your Own Answer*_____

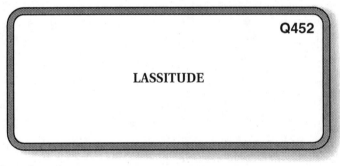

Q452

LASSITUDE

*Your Own Answer*_____

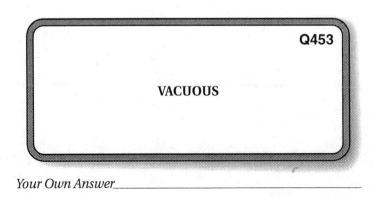

Q453

VACUOUS

*Your Own Answer*_____

Correct Answers

n.—foolhardiness; recklessness
Temerity can result in tragedy.

n.—weariness
Ten days of continual work caused a feeling of
lassitude for the worker.

adj.—dull; stupid; empty-headed
Test results showed him to be a **vacuous** person.

Questions

Q454

ABYSSAL

*Your Own Answer*_____

Q455

UNEQUIVOCAL

*Your Own Answer*_____

Q456

ABERRANT

*Your Own Answer*_____

Correct Answers

A454

adj.—of or relating to the deepest portions of the oceans

Thanks to thermal vents connected to the Earth's core, it turns out that even **abyssal** waters are able to support a rich array of life.

A455

adj.—clear and unambiguous

The 50-0 vote against the bill was an **unequivocal** statement against the measure.

A456

adj.—abnormal; straying from the normal or usual path

The **aberrant** flight pattern of the airplane alarmed the air traffic controllers.

Questions

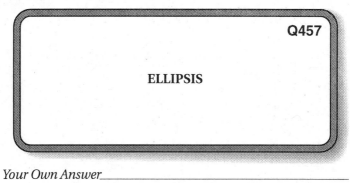

Q457

ELLIPSIS

*Your Own Answer*_____

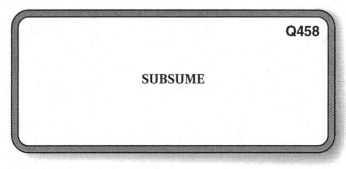

Q458

SUBSUME

*Your Own Answer*_____

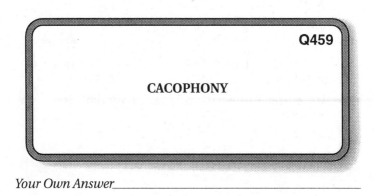

Q459

CACOPHONY

*Your Own Answer*_____

Correct Answers

n.—omission of words necessary for the complete syntactical construction of a sentence, but not necessary for understanding it

The **ellipsis** shortened the student's essay without eliminating any of the meaning.

v.—to include within a larger group

The AFL was **subsumed** by the NFL in the 1960s.

n.—a harsh, inharmonious collection of sounds; dissonance

The amateur band created more **cacophony** than beautiful sound.

Questions

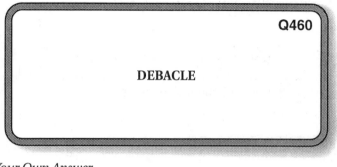

Q460

DEBACLE

*Your Own Answer*_____

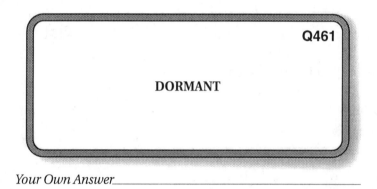

Q461

DORMANT

*Your Own Answer*_____

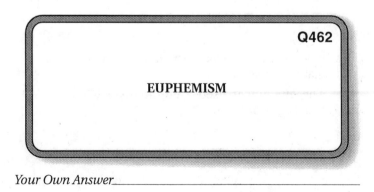

Q462

EUPHEMISM

*Your Own Answer*_____

Correct Answers

A460

n.—a disaster; a collapse; a rout

The American taxpayers are still paying the bill for the savings and loan **debacle**.

A461

adj.—as if asleep

The animals lay **dormant** until the spring thaw.

A462

n.—the use of a word or phrase in place of one that is distasteful

The announcer used a **euphemism** when he wanted to complain.

Questions

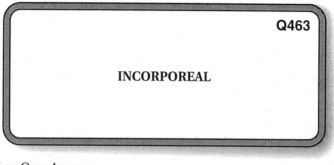

Q463

INCORPOREAL

*Your Own Answer*_____

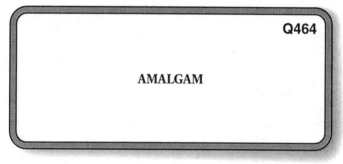

Q464

AMALGAM

*Your Own Answer*_____

Q465

VISAGE

*Your Own Answer*_____

Correct Answers

A463

adj.—not consisting of matter

The lake was so clear that it seemed **incorporeal**, and she had to dip her feet in before believing it was real.

A464

n.—a mixture or combination (often of metals)

The art display was an **amalgam** of modern and traditional pieces.

A465

n.—face; appearance

The artist's **visage** was often included in her paintings.

Questions

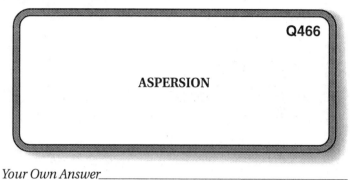

Q466

ASPERSION

*Your Own Answer*_____

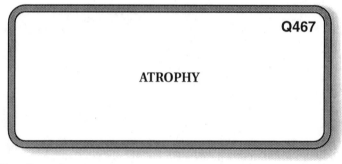

Q467

ATROPHY

*Your Own Answer*_____

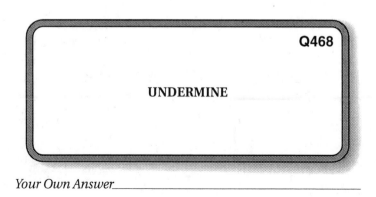

Q468

UNDERMINE

*Your Own Answer*_____

Correct Answers

n.—slanderous statement; a damaging or derogatory criticism

The **aspersion** damaged the credibility of the organization.

n.—wasting away, as from lack of use; failure to grow

The **atrophy** of the muscles was due to injury.

v.—to weaken, often through subtle means

The attempts to **undermine** the merger were unsuccessful.

Questions

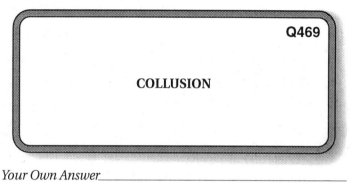

Q469

COLLUSION

*Your Own Answer*_____

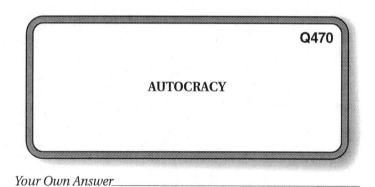

Q470

AUTOCRACY

*Your Own Answer*_____

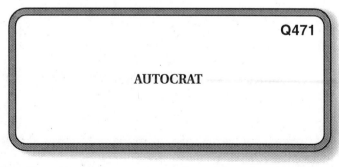

Q471

AUTOCRAT

*Your Own Answer*_____

Correct Answers

A469

n.—a secret agreement for an illegal purpose

The authorities discovered **collusion** between the director and treasurer.

A470

n.—an absolute monarchy; government where one person holds power

The **autocracy** was headed by a demanding man.

A471

n.—an absolute ruler

The **autocrat** in charge of the government was a man of power and prestige.

Questions

Q472

IMPLACABLE

*Your Own Answer*_____

Q473

ACERBIC

*Your Own Answer*_____

Q474

EPITOME

*Your Own Answer*_____

Correct Answers

A472

adj.—unwilling to be pacified or appeased

The baby was so **implacable** that a warm bottle would not settle her.

A473

adj.—sour or bitter in taste or manner

The baby's mouth puckered when she was given the **acerbic** medicine.

A474

n.—a part that is typical of the whole

The ballet dancer was the **epitome** of beauty and grace.

Questions

Q475

STIPEND

*Your Own Answer*_____

Q476

FEALTY

*Your Own Answer*_____

Q477

BAROQUE

*Your Own Answer*_____

Correct Answers

A475

n.—a fixed payment

The bank will pay the woman a **stipend** of a hundred dollars per week.

A476

n.—loyalty

The baron was given land in exchange for his **fealty** to the king.

A477

adj.—embellished; ornate

The **baroque** furnishings did not fit in the plain, modest home.

Questions

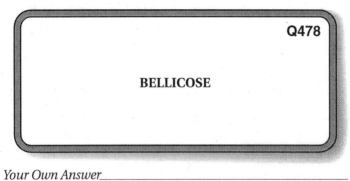

Q478

BELLICOSE

*Your Own Answer*_____

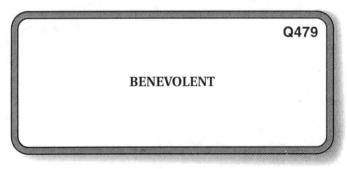

Q479

BENEVOLENT

*Your Own Answer*_____

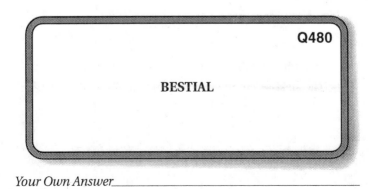

Q480

BESTIAL

*Your Own Answer*_____

Correct Answers

A478

adj.—quarrelsome; warlike

The **bellicose** guest would not be invited back again.

A479

adj.—kindly

The **benevolent** gentleman volunteered his services.

A480

adj.—having the qualities of a beast; brutal

The **bestial** employer made his employees work in an unheated room.

Questions

Q481

BLIGHTED

*Your Own Answer*_____

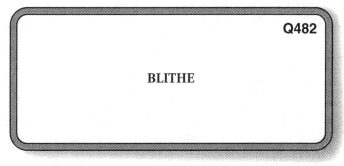

Q482

BLITHE

*Your Own Answer*_____

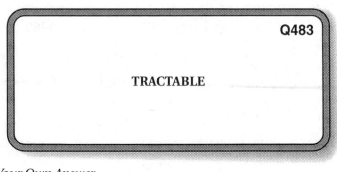

Q483

TRACTABLE

*Your Own Answer*_____

Correct Answers

A481

v.—causing frustration or destruction

The tornado **blighted** the town, leaving only one building standing.

A482

adj.—cheerful

The **blithe** child was a pleasant surprise.

A483

adj.—easily managed (opposite: intractable)

The boat was so lightweight it was **tractable** by one person.

Questions

Q484

ALLEGORY

*Your Own Answer*_____

_____

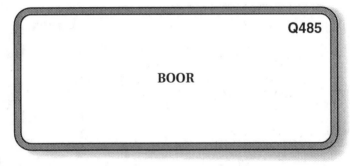

Q485

BOOR

*Your Own Answer*_____

_____

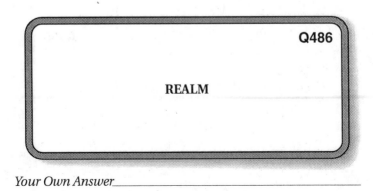

Q486

REALM

*Your Own Answer*_____

_____

Correct Answers

A484

n.—a literary, dramatic, or pictorial representation that is symbolic

The "Ugly Duckling" is an **allegory** which teaches a valuable lesson.

A485

n.—a rude person

The **boor** was not invited to the party, but he came anyway.

A486

n.—a region

The bounding islands were added to the **realm** of the kingdom.

Questions

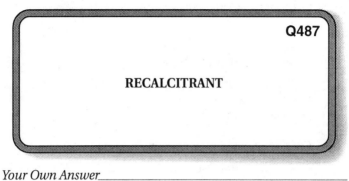

Q487

RECALCITRANT

*Your Own Answer*_____

Q488

NETTLE

*Your Own Answer*_____

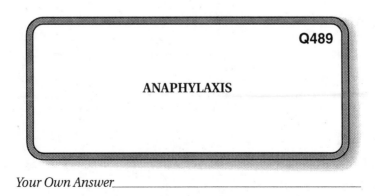

Q489

ANAPHYLAXIS

*Your Own Answer*_____

Correct Answers

A487

adj.—stubbornly rebellious
The boy became **recalcitrant** when the curfew was enforced.

A488

v.—to irritate
The boy will **nettle** his father into agreeing.

A489

n.—an allergic reaction
The boy's severe **anaphylaxis** to a series of medications made writing prescriptions a tricky proposition.

Questions

BILATERAL

*Your Own Answer*_____

COALESCE

*Your Own Answer*_____

BUCOLIC

*Your Own Answer*_____

Correct Answers

A490

adj.—two-sided
The brain is a **bilateral** organ, consisting of left
and right hemispheres.

A491

v.—to grow together; to combine
The bride and groom **coalesced** their funds to increase their collateral.

A492

adj.—having to do with shepherds or the country
The **bucolic** setting inspired the artist.

Questions

Q493

EXTRAPOLATE

*Your Own Answer*_____

Q494

SUBJUGATE

*Your Own Answer*_____

Q495

CACHE

*Your Own Answer*_____

Correct Answers

A493

v.—to estimate the value of something beyond the scale; to infer what is unknown from something known

The budget for the next five years was **extrapolated** from that year's data.

A494

v.—to dominate or enslave

The bully will attempt to **subjugate** the remainder of the class.

A495

n.—a safe place for hiding

The **cache** for his jewelry was under the bed.

Questions

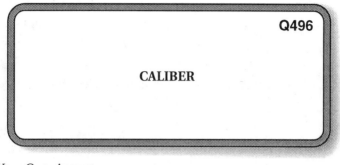

Q496

CALIBER

*Your Own Answer*_____

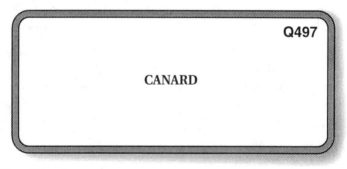

Q497

CANARD

*Your Own Answer*_____

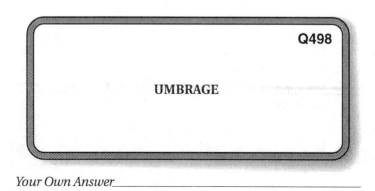

Q498

UMBRAGE

*Your Own Answer*_____

Correct Answers

A496

n.—quality

The **caliber** of talent at the show was excellent.

A497

n.—a false statement or rumor

The **canard** was reported in a scandalous tabloid.

A498

n.—offense or resentment

The candidate took **umbrage** at the remark of his opponent.

Questions

Q499

COMPLACENT

*Your Own Answer*_____

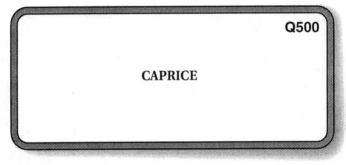

Q500

CAPRICE

*Your Own Answer*_____

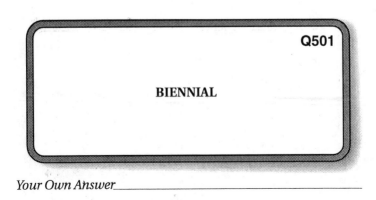

Q501

BIENNIAL

*Your Own Answer*_____

Correct Answers

A499

adj.—self-satisfied; content

The candidate was so **complacent** with his poll numbers that he virtually stopped campaigning.

A500

n.—a sudden, unpredictable, or whimsical change

She was known for her **caprice**, always changing her plans from minute to minute.

A501

adj.—occurring every two years

The celebration was a **biennial** event.

Questions

Q502

DANK

*Your Own Answer*_____

Q503

CESSATION

*Your Own Answer*_____

Q504

HARMONIOUS

*Your Own Answer*_____

Correct Answers

A502

adj.—damp and chilly
The cellar became very **dank** during the winter-time.

A503

n.—a ceasing; a stopping
The **cessation** of a bad habit is often difficult to sustain.

A504

adj.—having proportionate and orderly parts
The challenge for the new conductor was to mesh her musicians' talent into a **harmonious** orches-tra.

Questions

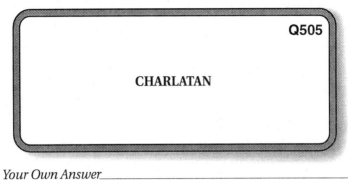

Q505

CHARLATAN

*Your Own Answer*_____

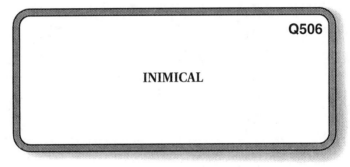

Q506

INIMICAL

*Your Own Answer*_____

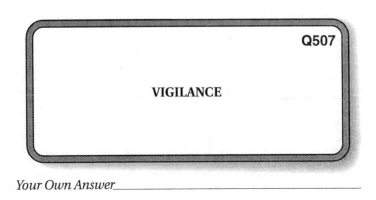

Q507

VIGILANCE

*Your Own Answer*_____

Correct Answers

n.—a person who pretends to have knowledge
The **charlatan** deceived the townspeople.

adj.—hostile; unfriendly
The chess player directed an **inimical** stare at his opponent to knock him off his game.

n.—watchfulness
The child could not escape the **vigilance** of his mother's eyes.

Questions

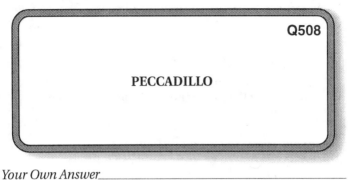

Q508

PECCADILLO

*Your Own Answer*_____

_____

Q509

IMPERVIOUS

*Your Own Answer*_____

_____

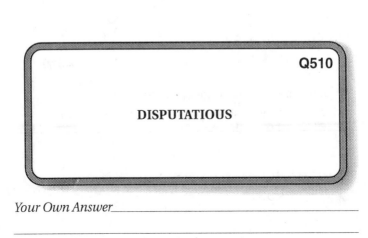

Q510

DISPUTATIOUS

*Your Own Answer*_____

_____

Correct Answers

A508

n.—a slight fault or offense

The child was embarrassed when he was caught committing the **peccadillo** of eating chocolate before dinner.

A509

adj.—impenetrable; not allowing anything to pass through; unaffected

Her new coat was **impervious** to the rain.

A510

adj.—argumentative; inclined to disputes

The child was so **disputatious** he needed to be removed from the room.

Questions

Q511

CAVIL

*Your Own Answer*_____

Q512

BEHOLDEN

*Your Own Answer*_____

Q513

CHOLERIC

*Your Own Answer*_____

Correct Answers

A511

v.—to bicker unnecessarily
The mother and daughter often **caviled** over trivial matters.

A512

adj.—indebted to
The children were **beholden** to their parents for their car loans.

A513

adj.—ill-tempered; easily angered
The children were afraid of the **choleric** neighbor because he always yelled at them for being too loud.

Questions

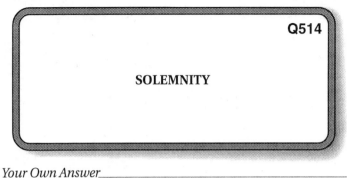

Q514

SOLEMNITY

*Your Own Answer*_____

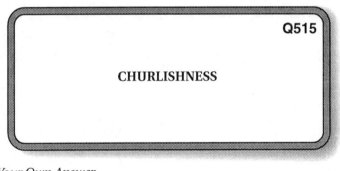

Q515

CHURLISHNESS

*Your Own Answer*_____

Q516

MUNIFICENT

*Your Own Answer*_____

Correct Answers

A514

n.—a deep, reverent feeling often associated with religious occasions

The church service was full of **solemnity**.

A515

n.—crude or surly behavior

The **churlishness** of the teenager caused his employer to lose faith in him.

A516

adj.—showing great generosity

The civic group made a **munificent** donation to the homeless shelter.

Questions

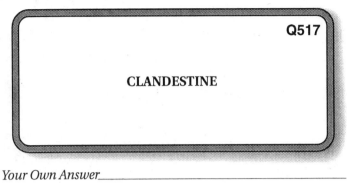

Q517

CLANDESTINE

*Your Own Answer*_____

_____

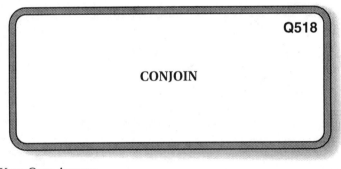

Q518

CONJOIN

*Your Own Answer*_____

_____

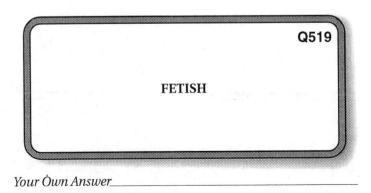

Q519

FETISH

*Your Own Answer*_____

_____

Correct Answers

adj.—secret

The **clandestine** plan must be kept between the two of us!

v.—to combine

The classes will **conjoin** to do the play.

n.—anything to which one gives excessive devotion

The clay figure of a fertility goddess was a **fetish** from an ancient civilization.

Questions

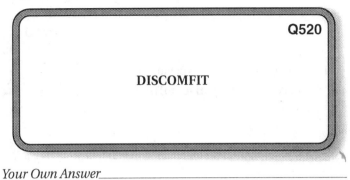

Q520

DISCOMFIT

*Your Own Answer*_____

_____

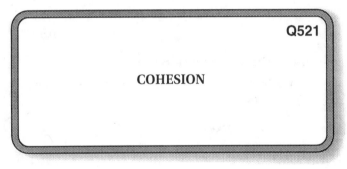

Q521

COHESION

*Your Own Answer*_____

_____

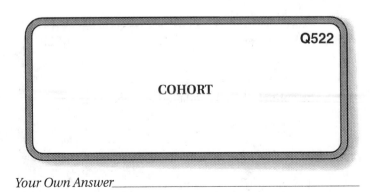

Q522

COHORT

*Your Own Answer*_____

_____

Correct Answers

A520

v.—to frustrate the expectations of
The close game **discomfited** the number one player.

A521

n.—the act of holding together
The **cohesion** of the group increased as friendships were formed.

A522

n.—a group; a band
The **cohort** of teens gathered at the athletic field.

Questions

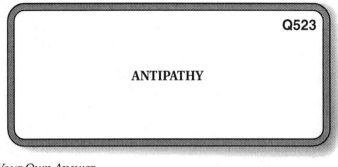

Q523

ANTIPATHY

*Your Own Answer*_____

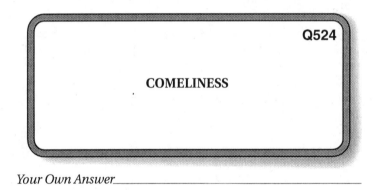

Q524

COMELINESS

*Your Own Answer*_____

Q525

FRAUGHT

*Your Own Answer*_____

Correct Answers

A523

n.—a strong dislike or repugnance

The colonies' **antipathy** toward the British stemmed in large part from burdensome taxes.

A524

n.—beauty; attractiveness in appearance or behavior

The **comeliness** of the woman attracted everyone's attention.

A525

adj.—loaded; charged

The comment was **fraught** with sarcasm.

Questions

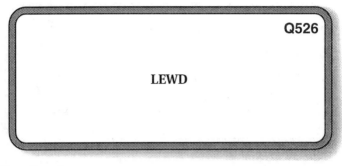

Q526

LEWD

*Your Own Answer*_____

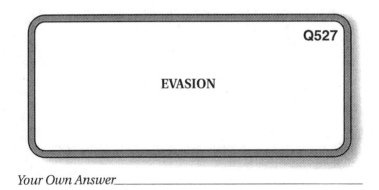

Q527

EVASION

*Your Own Answer*_____

Q528

COMPLAISANCE

*Your Own Answer*_____

Correct Answers

A526

adj.—lustful; wicked

The comment was so **lewd** that it could not be repeated in front of children.

A527

n.—the avoiding of a duty

The company was charged with tax **evasion** as it did not pay all that it owed.

A528

n.—the quality of being agreeable or eager to please

The **complaisance** of the woman was a quality which made many people like her.

Questions

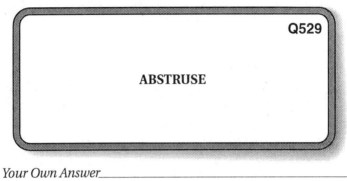

Q529

ABSTRUSE

*Your Own Answer*_____

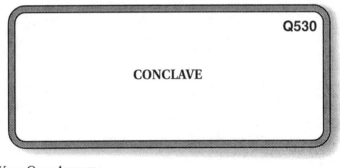

Q530

CONCLAVE

*Your Own Answer*_____

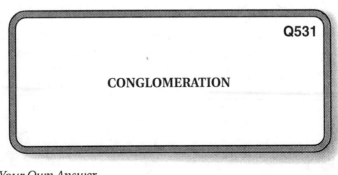

Q531

CONGLOMERATION

*Your Own Answer*_____

Correct Answers

A529

adj.—hard to understand

The concept was too **abstruse** for the average first-year student to grasp.

A530

n.—any private meeting or closed assembly

The **conclave** was to meet in the executive suite.

A531

n.—a collection or mixture of various things

The **conglomeration** is made up of four different interest groups.

Questions

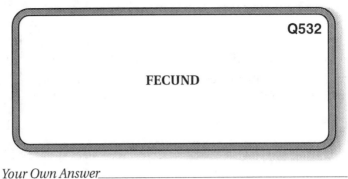

Q532

FECUND

*Your Own Answer*_____

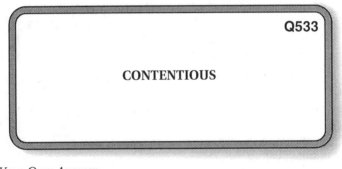

Q533

CONTENTIOUS

*Your Own Answer*_____

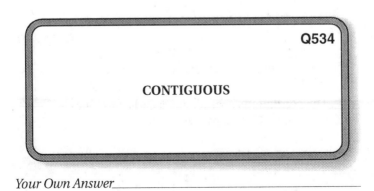

Q534

CONTIGUOUS

*Your Own Answer*_____

Correct Answers

adj.—productive

The construction crew had a **fecund** day and was able to leave early.

adj.—quarrelsome

The **contentious** student was asked to leave the classroom.

adj.—touching or adjoining and close, but not touching

The **contiguous** apartment was home to four cats which could be heard meowing.

Questions

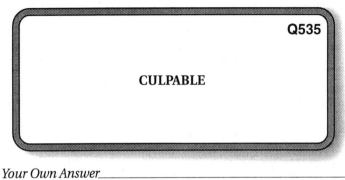

Q535

CULPABLE

*Your Own Answer*_____

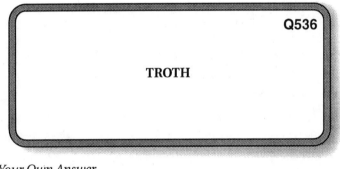

Q536

TROTH

*Your Own Answer*_____

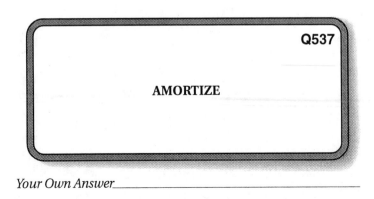

Q537

AMORTIZE

*Your Own Answer*_____

Correct Answers

A535

adj.—deserving blame; guilty

The convicted criminal still denies that he is **culpable** for the robbery.

A536

n.—belief; faith; fidelity

The couple pledged **troth** to each other through their vows.

A537

v.—to liquidate (a debt) at fixed intervals

The couple **amortized** their mortgage sooner than they expected.

Questions

Q538

MENDACIOUS

*Your Own Answer*_____

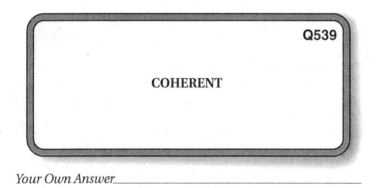

Q539

COHERENT

*Your Own Answer*_____

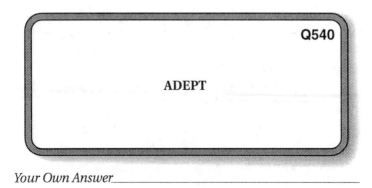

Q540

ADEPT

*Your Own Answer*_____

Correct Answers

A538

adj.—not truthful; lying

The couple was swindled out its life's savings by the **mendacious** con men.

A539

adj.—sticking together; connected; logical; consistent

The course was a success due to its **coherent** information.

A540

adj.—skilled; practiced

The craftsman was **adept** at creating beautiful vases and candleholders.

Questions

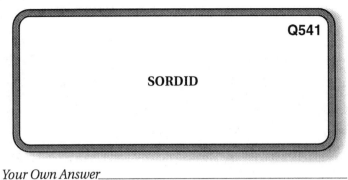

Q541

SORDID

*Your Own Answer*_____

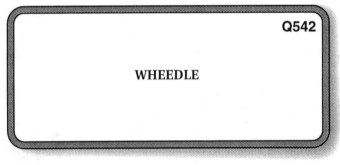

Q542

WHEEDLE

*Your Own Answer*_____

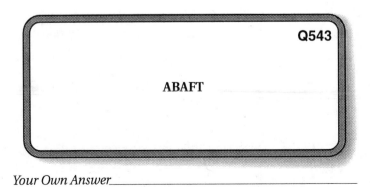

Q543

ABAFT

*Your Own Answer*_____

Correct Answers

A541

adj.—filthy; foul

The criminal's thought patterns were so **sordid** that he was not granted parole.

A542

v.—to influence or persuade by flattery

The politician may attempt to **wheedle** votes from the citizens.

A543

adv.—on or toward the rear of a ship

The cruise passengers moved **abaft** to soak up the Caribbean sun poolside.

Questions

Q544

CURMUDGEON

*Your Own Answer*_____

Q545

DAIS

*Your Own Answer*_____

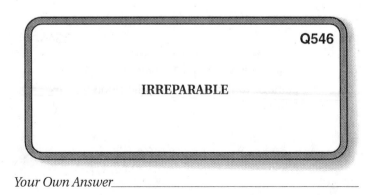

Q546

IRREPARABLE

*Your Own Answer*_____

Correct Answers

A544

n.—an ill-tempered person

The **curmudgeon** asked the children not to play near the house.

A545

n.—a raised platform at one end of a room

The **dais** was lowered to make the speaker look taller.

A546

adj.—that which cannot be repaired or regained

The damage to the house after the flood was **irreparable**.

Questions

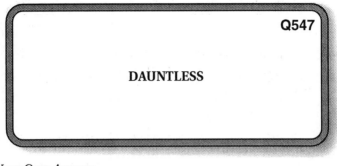

Q547

DAUNTLESS

*Your Own Answer*_____

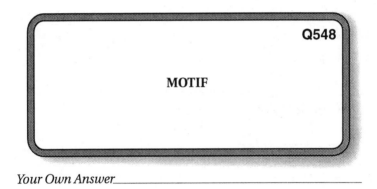

Q548

MOTIF

*Your Own Answer*_____

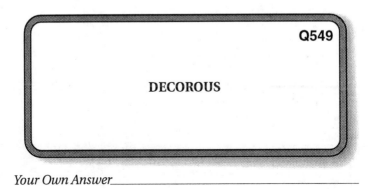

Q549

DECOROUS

*Your Own Answer*_____

Correct Answers

A547

adj.—fearless; not discouraged

The **dauntless** ranger scaled the mountain to complete the rescue.

A548

n.—a repeated figure or design in architecture or decoration

The woman loved her roses and made the flower the **motif** of her decorations.

A549

adj.—suitable; proper; seemly

The employer was impressed by the applicant's **decorous** manner.

Questions

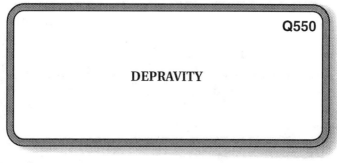

Q550

DEPRAVITY

*Your Own Answer*_____

_____

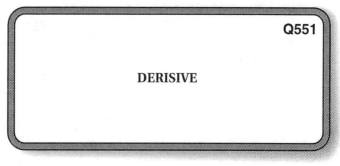

Q551

DERISIVE

*Your Own Answer*_____

_____

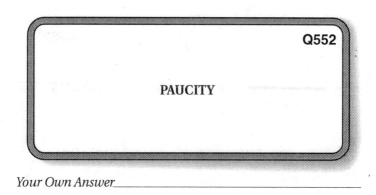

Q552

PAUCITY

*Your Own Answer*_____

_____

Correct Answers

A550

n.—wickedness
The **depravity** of the old man was bound to land him in jail one day.

A551

adj.—showing disrespect or scorn for
The **derisive** comment was aimed at the man's life-long enemy.

A552

n.—scarcity
The described feast was actually a buffet with a **paucity** of food.

Questions

Q553

CARTE BLANCHE

*Your Own Answer*_____

_____

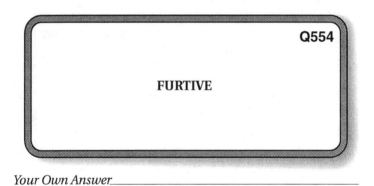

Q554

FURTIVE

*Your Own Answer*_____

_____

Q555

CURSORY

*Your Own Answer*_____

_____

Correct Answers

A553

n.—unlimited authority

The designer was given **carte blanche** to create a new line for the fall.

A554

adj.—secretive; sly

The detective had much difficulty finding the **furtive** criminal.

A555

adj.—hasty

The detective's **cursory** examination of the crime scene caused him to overlook the lesser clues.

Questions

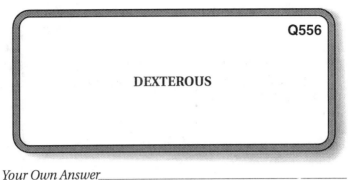

Q556

DEXTEROUS

*Your Own Answer*_____

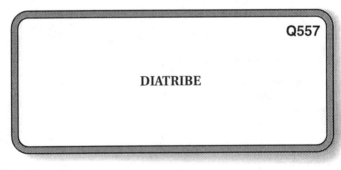

Q557

DIATRIBE

*Your Own Answer*_____

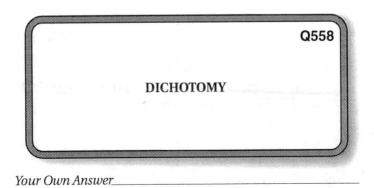

Q558

DICHOTOMY

*Your Own Answer*_____

Correct Answers

A556

adj.—skillful; quick mentally or physically

The **dexterous** gymnast was the epitome of grace on the balance beam.

A557

n.—a bitter or abusive speech

The **diatribe** was directed towards a disrespectful supervisor.

A558

n.—a division into two parts

The **dichotomy** between church and state renders school prayer unconstitutional.

Questions

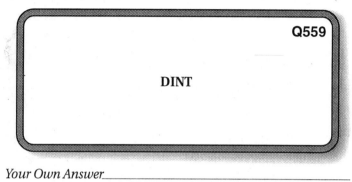

Q559

DINT

*Your Own Answer*_____

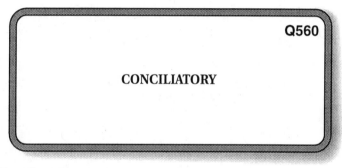

Q560

CONCILIATORY

*Your Own Answer*_____

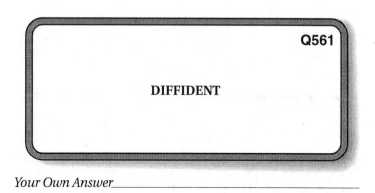

Q561

DIFFIDENT

*Your Own Answer*_____

Correct Answers

A559

n.—force; exertion

The lawyer won the case by **dint** of argument.

A560

adj.—tending to reconcile

The diplomat sought to take a **conciliatory** approach to keep the talks going.

A561

adj.—timid; lacking self-confidence

The director is looking for a self-assured actor, not a **diffident** one.

Questions

Q562

DISINGENUOUS

*Your Own Answer*_____

Q563

MOOT

*Your Own Answer*_____

Q564

DISPARATE

*Your Own Answer*_____

Correct Answers

A562

adj.—not frank or candid; deceivingly simple (opposite: ingenuous)

The director used a **disingenuous** remark to make his point to the student.

A563

adj.—subject to or open for discussion or debate

The discussion of extending the girl's curfew was a **moot** point.

A564

adj.—unequal; dissimilar; different

The **disparate** numbers of players made the game a sure blowout.

Questions

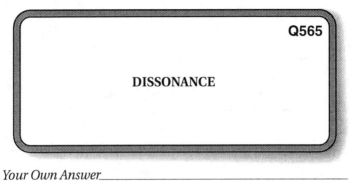

Q565

DISSONANCE

*Your Own Answer*_____

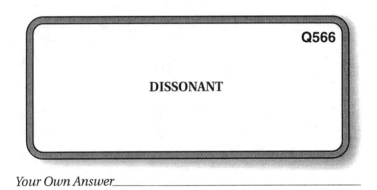

Q566

DISSONANT

*Your Own Answer*_____

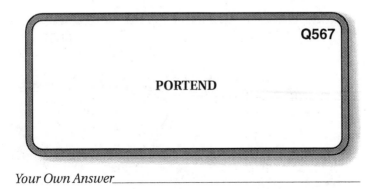

Q567

PORTEND

*Your Own Answer*_____

Correct Answers

A565

n.—musical discord; a mingling of inharmonious sounds; disagreement; lack of harmony

The **dissonance** of his composition makes for some painful listening.

A566

adj.—not in harmony; in disagreement

The **dissonant** nature of the man's temperament made the woman fearful to approach him with the new idea.

A567

v.—to be an omen of; signify

The distant roll of thunder **portends** an oncoming storm.

Questions

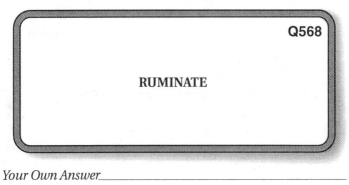

Q568

RUMINATE

*Your Own Answer*_____

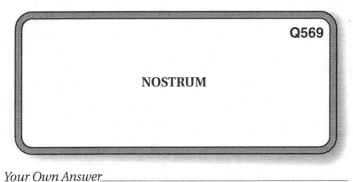

Q569

NOSTRUM

*Your Own Answer*_____

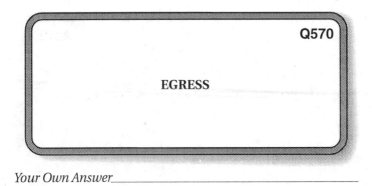

Q570

EGRESS

*Your Own Answer*_____

Correct Answers

A568

v.—to consider carefully
The doctor will **ruminate** on his diagnosis.

A569

n.—a questionable remedy
The doctor's prescription was so unusual that it could be considered a **nostrum**.

A570

n.—a way out; exit
The doorway provided an **egress** from the chamber.

Questions

Q571

DOUGHTY

*Your Own Answer*_____

_____

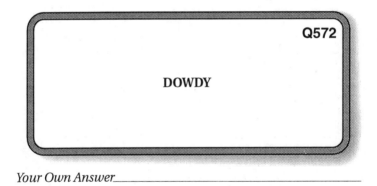

Q572

DOWDY

*Your Own Answer*_____

_____

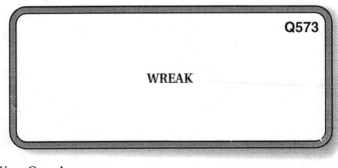

Q573

WREAK

*Your Own Answer*_____

_____

Correct Answers

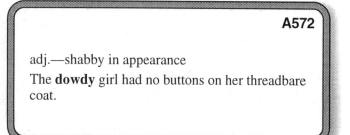

A571

adj.—brave
The **doughty** fireman saved the woman's life.

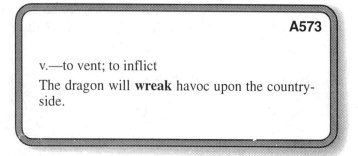

A572

adj.—shabby in appearance
The **dowdy** girl had no buttons on her threadbare coat.

A573

v.—to vent; to inflict
The dragon will **wreak** havoc upon the country-side.

Questions

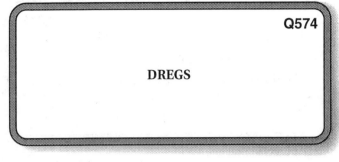

Q574

DREGS

*Your Own Answer*_____

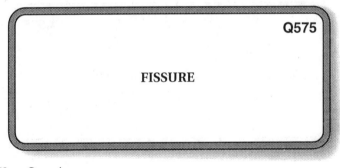

Q575

FISSURE

*Your Own Answer*_____

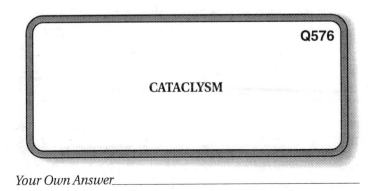

Q576

CATACLYSM

*Your Own Answer*_____

Correct Answers

A574

n.—the unwanted part

The **dregs** of the meal were given to the family pet.

A575

n.—a cleft or crack

The earthquake caused a **fissure** which split the cliff face.

A576

n.—a great upheaval; violent change, such as an earthquake or a war

The earthquake has been the first **cataclysm** in five years.

Questions

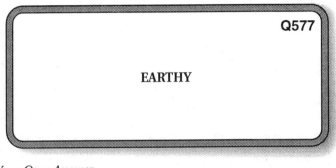

Q577

EARTHY

*Your Own Answer*_____

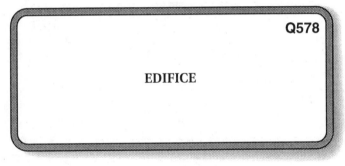

Q578

EDIFICE

*Your Own Answer*_____

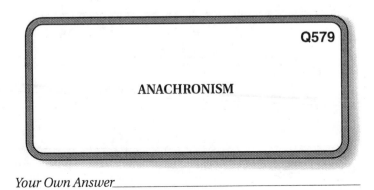

Q579

ANACHRONISM

*Your Own Answer*_____

Correct Answers

adj.—unrefined

The **earthy**-looking table was bare.

n.—a large building

The **edifice** rose twenty stories and spanned two blocks.

n.—something out of place in time (e.g., a computer in medieval times)

The editor recognized an **anachronism** in the manuscript where a character living in 1902 boards an airplane.

Questions

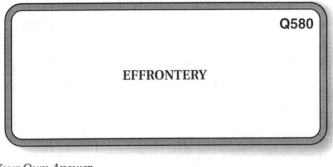

Q580

EFFRONTERY

*Your Own Answer*_____

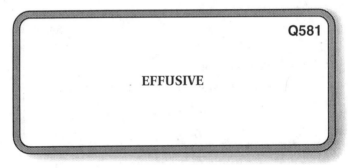

Q581

EFFUSIVE

*Your Own Answer*_____

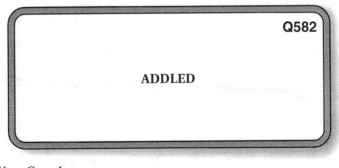

Q582

ADDLED

*Your Own Answer*_____

Correct Answers

A580

n.—shameless boldness
The **effrontery** of the young man was offensive.

A581

adj.—pouring out or forth; overflowing
The **effusive** currents rush through the broken dam.

A582

adj.—rotten
The egg will become **addled** if it is left un-
refrigerated.

Questions

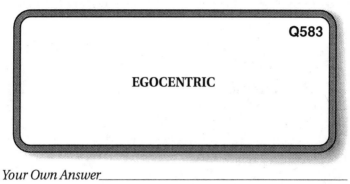

Q583

EGOCENTRIC

*Your Own Answer*_____

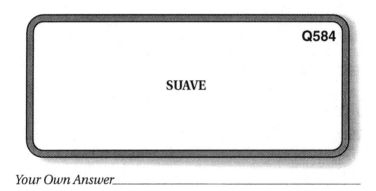

Q584

SUAVE

*Your Own Answer*_____

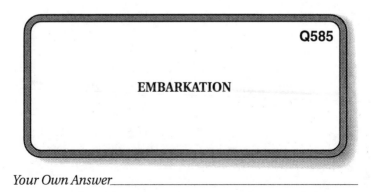

Q585

EMBARKATION

*Your Own Answer*_____

Correct Answers

A583

adj.—self-centered; viewing everything in relation to oneself

The **egocentric** professor could not accept the students' opinions as valid.

A584

adj.—polished

Everyone noticed the **suave** woman when she entered the room.

A585

n.—the act of engaging or investing in

The **embarkation** into self-employment was a new start for the woman.

Questions

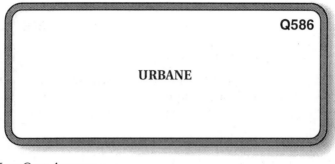

Q586

URBANE

*Your Own Answer*_____

_____

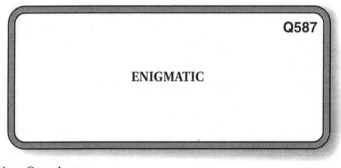

Q587

ENIGMATIC

*Your Own Answer*_____

_____

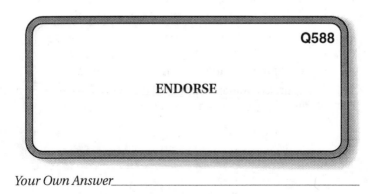

Q588

ENDORSE

*Your Own Answer*_____

_____

Correct Answers

A586

adj.—a polished way of acting
The English businessman was described by his peers as witty and **urbane**.

A587

adj.—baffling
The **enigmatic** murder case plagued the detective.

A588

v.—to support; to approve of; to recommend
The entire community **endorsed** the politician who promised lower taxes and a better school system.

Questions

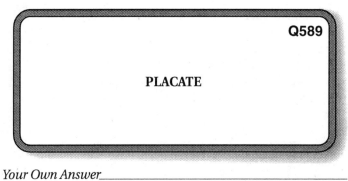

Q589

PLACATE

*Your Own Answer*_____

_____

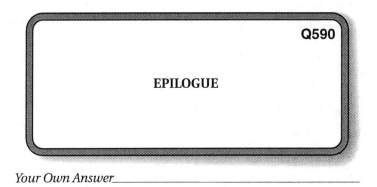

Q590

EPILOGUE

*Your Own Answer*_____

_____

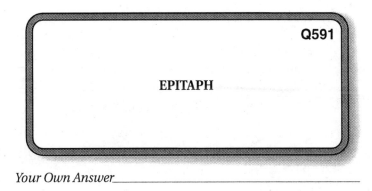

Q591

EPITAPH

*Your Own Answer*_____

_____

Correct Answers

A589

v.—to appease or pacify

The entire family attempted to **placate** the stubborn child.

A590

n.—the closing section of a play or novel providing further comment

The **epilogue** told us the destiny of the characters.

A591

n.—an inscription on a monument in honor or memory of a dead person

The **epitaph** described the actions of a brave man.

Questions

Q592

EQUIVOCATION

*Your Own Answer*_____

Q593

ESTIMABLE

*Your Own Answer*_____

Q594

EULOGY

*Your Own Answer*_____

Correct Answers

A592

n.—a purposely misleading statement

The **equivocation** by the man sent the search team looking in the wrong direction.

A593

adj.—deserving respect

The **estimable** hero was given a parade.

A594

n.—words of praise, especially for the dead

The **eulogy** was a remembrance of the good things the man accomplished in his lifetime.

Questions

Q595

EUPHONY

*Your Own Answer*_____

Q596

EVANESCENT

*Your Own Answer*_____

Q597

FROWARD

*Your Own Answer*_____

Correct Answers

A595

n.—pleasant sound

The **euphony** created by the orchestra was due to years of practice.

A596

adj.—vanishing quickly; dissipating like a vapor

She wasn't given enough time to examine the **evanescent** image.

A597

adj.—not willing to yield or comply with what is reasonable

The executive had to deal wth a **froward** peer who was becoming increasingly difficult.

Questions

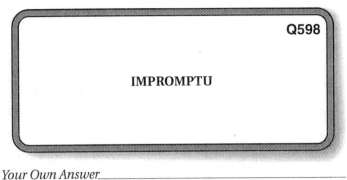

Q598

IMPROMPTU

*Your Own Answer*_____

_____

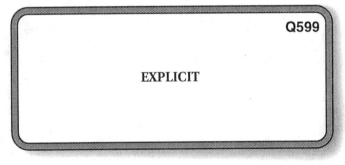

Q599

EXPLICIT

*Your Own Answer*_____

_____

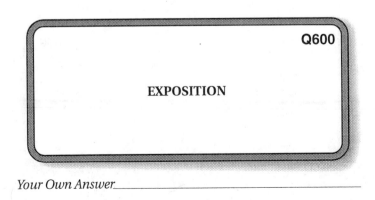

Q600

EXPOSITION

*Your Own Answer*_____

_____

Correct Answers

A598

adj.—without advanced thought
The executive needed to make an **impromptu** speech.

A599

adj.—specific; definite
They couldn't comprehend why she was lost because they gave her **explicit** directions.

A600

n.—a setting forth of facts
The **exposition** by the witness substantiated the story given by the prisoner.

Questions

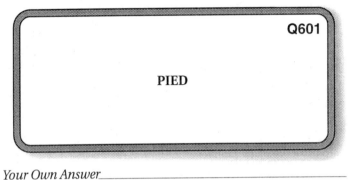

Q601

PIED

*Your Own Answer*_____

_____

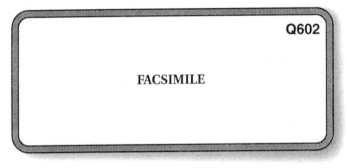

Q602

FACSIMILE

*Your Own Answer*_____

_____

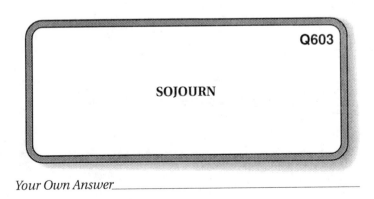

Q603

SOJOURN

*Your Own Answer*_____

_____

Correct Answers

A601

adj.—patchy in color
The bird's **pied** feathers were lovely to look at.

A602

n.—copy; reproduction; replica
The **facsimile** of the elaborate painting was indistinguishable from the original.

A603

v.—to stay temporarily
The family will **sojourn** at their summer home.

Questions

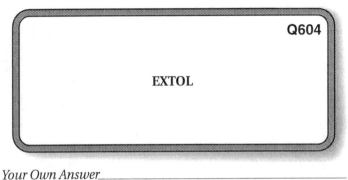

Q604

EXTOL

*Your Own Answer*_____

_____

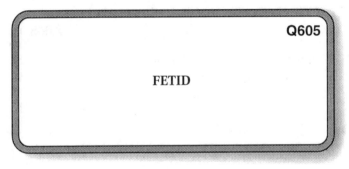

Q605

FETID

*Your Own Answer*_____

_____

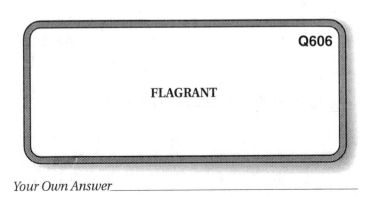

Q606

FLAGRANT

*Your Own Answer*_____

_____

Correct Answers

A604

v.—to give great praise
The father will **extol** the success of his son to everyone he meets.

A605

adj.—having an offensive smell
The **fetid** air led us to believe something was decaying in the basement.

A606

adj.—glaringly wrong
The **flagrant** foul was apparent to everyone.

Questions

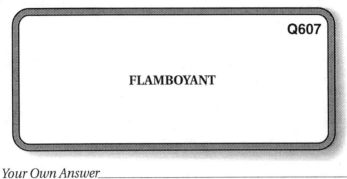

Q607

FLAMBOYANT

*Your Own Answer*_____

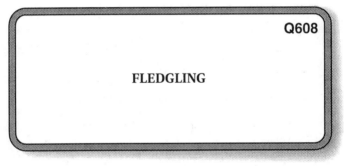

Q608

FLEDGLING

*Your Own Answer*_____

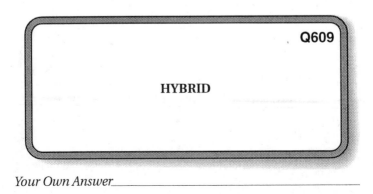

Q609

HYBRID

*Your Own Answer*_____

Correct Answers

A607

adj.—being too showy or ornate

The **flamboyant** nature of the couple was evident in their loud clothing.

A608

n.—inexperienced person; beginner

The **fledgling** mountain climber needed assistance from the more experienced mountaineers.

A609

n.—anything of mixed origin

The flower was a **hybrid** of three different flowers.

Questions

Q610

LUCENT

*Your Own Answer*_____

Q611

MELLIFLUOUS

*Your Own Answer*_____

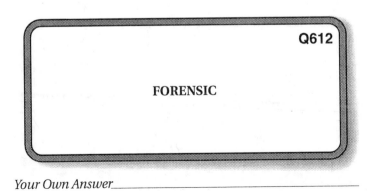

Q612

FORENSIC

*Your Own Answer*_____

Correct Answers

adj.—shining; translucent

The flowing garment gave the woman a **lucent** quality when standing in the spotlight.

adj.—having a sweet sound

The flute had a beautiful **mellifluous** sound.

adj.—pertaining to legal or public argument

The blood-stained glove could be used as **foren-sic** evidence in the murder case.

Questions

Q613

FORMIDABLE

*Your Own Answer*_____

Q614

FUSTIAN

*Your Own Answer*_____

Q615

OMNISCIENT

*Your Own Answer*_____

Correct Answers

A613

adj.—causing dread or fear
The **formidable** team caused weak knees in their opponents.

A614

n.—pompous talk or writing
The **fustian** of the professor discouraged the student from attending class.

A615

adj.—having knowledge of all things
The future can be told by the **omniscient** woman.

Questions

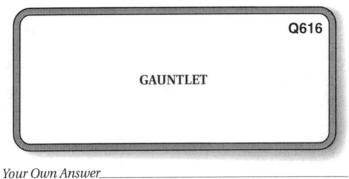

Q616

GAUNTLET

Your Own Answer

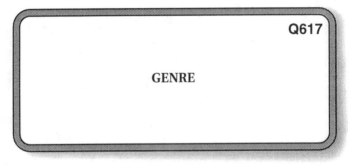

Q617

GENRE

Your Own Answer

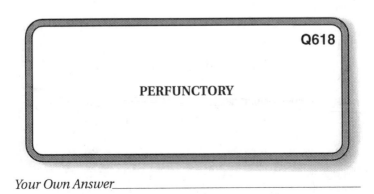

Q618

PERFUNCTORY

Your Own Answer

Correct Answers

A616

n.—a protective glove

The **gauntlet** saved the man's hand from being burned in the fire.

A617

n.—a type of film or book

The **genre** of the book is historical fiction.

A618

adj.—done in a routine, mechanical way, without interest

She performed her job in such a **perfunctory** manner that it soon became boring.

Questions

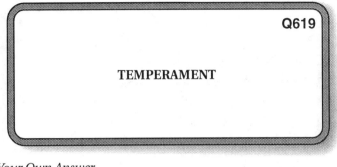

Q619

TEMPERAMENT

*Your Own Answer*_____

_____

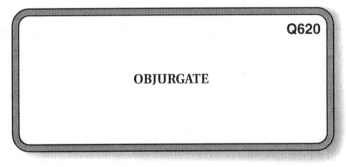

Q620

OBJURGATE

*Your Own Answer*_____

_____

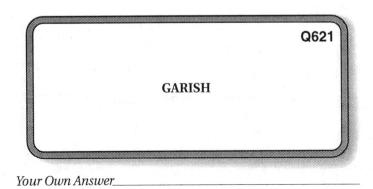

Q621

GARISH

*Your Own Answer*_____

_____

Correct Answers

A619

n.—one's customary frame of mind
The girl's **temperament** is usually very calm.

A620

v.—to chide vehemently
The teacher **objurgated** the misbehaved students.

A621

adj.—gaudy; showy
The gold fixtures seemed **garish**.

Questions

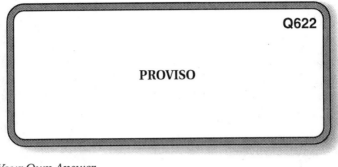

Q622

PROVISO

*Your Own Answer*_____

Q623

INDICT

*Your Own Answer*_____

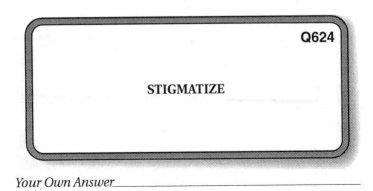

Q624

STIGMATIZE

*Your Own Answer*_____

Correct Answers

A622

n.—a clause stating a condition or stipulation

The governor began the conference with a **proviso** stating the disastrous results of the flood.

A623

v.—to formally accuse

The grand jury will **indict** the suspect when there is enough evidence.

A624

v.—to characterize or mark as disgraceful

The gross error will **stigmatize** the worker as careless.

Questions

ACQUIESCE

*Your Own Answer*_____

ENGENDER

*Your Own Answer*_____

HAPLESS

*Your Own Answer*_____

Correct Answers

A625

v.—to agree without protest

The group **acquiesced** to the new regulations even though they had fought them hammer and tongs.

A626

v.—to bring about; to beget; to bring forth

The group attempted to **engender** changes to the law.

A627

adj.—unlucky; unfortunate

The **hapless** team could not win a game.

Questions

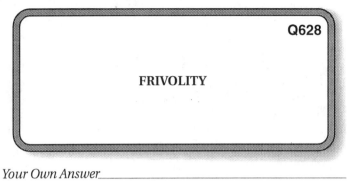

Q628

FRIVOLITY

*Your Own Answer*_____

_____

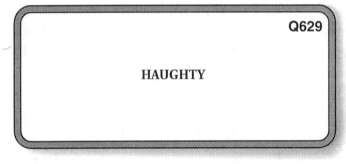

Q629

HAUGHTY

*Your Own Answer*_____

_____

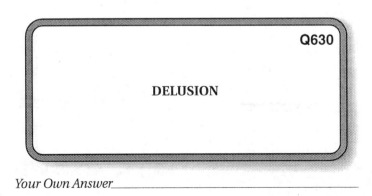

Q630

DELUSION

*Your Own Answer*_____

_____

Correct Answers

adj.—giddiness; lack of seriousness

The hard-working students deserved weekend gatherings filled with **frivolity**.

adj.—proud of oneself and scornful of others

Her **haughty** ways turned off her peers.

n.—a false belief or opinion

The historian suffered from the **delusion** that he was Napoleon.

Questions

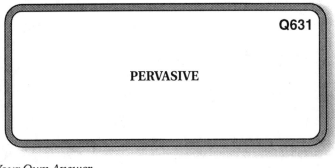

Q631

PERVASIVE

*Your Own Answer*_____

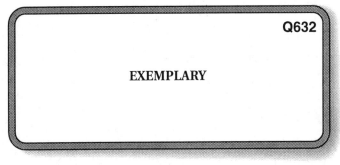

Q632

EXEMPLARY

*Your Own Answer*_____

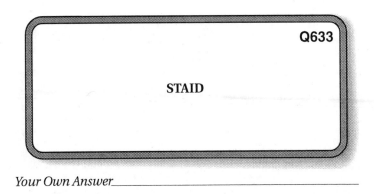

Q633

STAID

*Your Own Answer*_____

Correct Answers

adj.—spreading throughout

The home was filled with the **pervasive** aroma of baking bread.

adj.—serving as an example; outstanding

The honor student's **exemplary** behavior made him a role model to the younger children.

adj.—marked by self-control

Everyone was impressed by her **staid** manner, even while under extreme pressure.

Questions

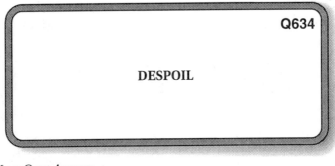

Q634

DESPOIL

*Your Own Answer*_____

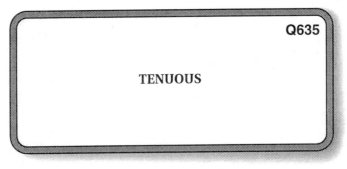

Q635

TENUOUS

*Your Own Answer*_____

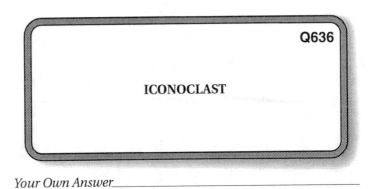

Q636

ICONOCLAST

*Your Own Answer*_____

Correct Answers

A634

v.—to take everything; to plunder

The Huns **despoiled** village after village.

A635

adj.—thin; slim; delicate; weak

The hurricane force winds ripped the **tenuous** branches from the tree.

A636

n.—one who smashes revered images; an attacker of cherished beliefs

The **iconoclast** spoke against the traditions of the holiday.

Questions

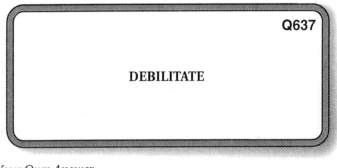

Q637

DEBILITATE

*Your Own Answer*_____

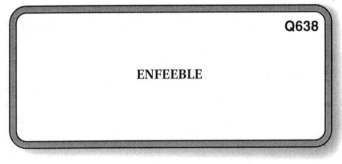

Q638

ENFEEBLE

*Your Own Answer*_____

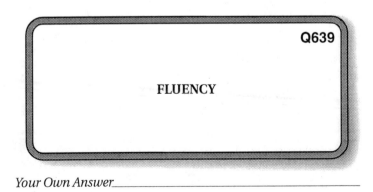

Q639

FLUENCY

*Your Own Answer*_____

Correct Answers

A637

v.—to make weak; to wear out
The illness will **debilitate** the muscles in his legs.

A638

v.—to make weak
The illness will **enfeeble** anyone who catches it.

A639

n.—smoothness of speech
The immigrant acquired **fluency** in English after studying for two years.

Questions

Q640

IMPERTURBABLE

*Your Own Answer*_____

Q641

IMPUTATION

*Your Own Answer*_____

Q642

INCHOATE

*Your Own Answer*_____

Correct Answers

A640

adj.—calm; not easily excited

The **imperturbable** man made an ideal negotiator.

A641

n.—charging or attributing a fault or misconduct to another

The **imputation** of guilt was made by the judge.

A642

adj.—not yet fully formed; rudimentary

The theory was rejected in its **inchoate** stages, but it was accepted in the end.

Questions

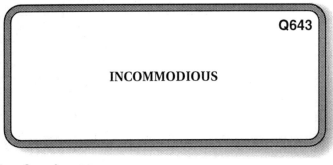

Q643

INCOMMODIOUS

*Your Own Answer*_____

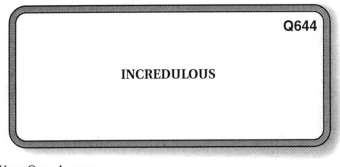

Q644

INCREDULOUS

*Your Own Answer*_____

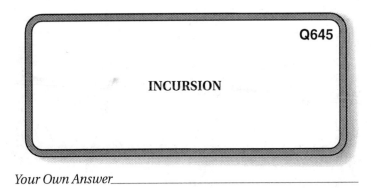

Q645

INCURSION

*Your Own Answer*_____

Correct Answers

adj.—inconvenient
The **incommodious** road detour caused her to miss an important interview.

adj.—skeptical
The **incredulous** look on his face led me to believe he was not convinced of its importance.

n.—an unfriendly entry; an invasion
The **incursion** by enemy forces left the country shocked.

Questions

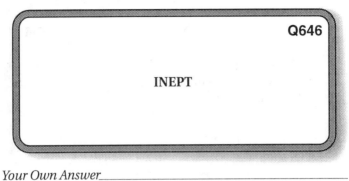

Q646

INEPT

*Your Own Answer*_____

Q647

INFAMOUS

*Your Own Answer*_____

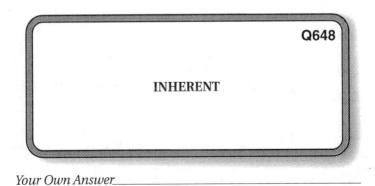

Q648

INHERENT

*Your Own Answer*_____

Correct Answers

A646

adj.—incompetent; clumsy
The **inept** clerk will never be promoted past the file room.

A647

adj.—having a bad reputation
The **infamous** gang was known for robbery.

A648

adj.—part of the essential character; intrinsic
The **inherent** desire to do well is present throughout the family.

Questions

Q649

INSOLVENT

*Your Own Answer*_____

Q650

INSULARITY

*Your Own Answer*_____

Q651

INTERMITTENT

*Your Own Answer*_____

Correct Answers

A649

adj.—unable to pay debts

The **insolvent** state of his bank account kept him from writing any checks.

A650

n.—having the characteristics of an island

The **insularity** of the country made it a great place to build a resort.

A651

adj.—stopping and starting at intervals

The **intermittent** light was distracting.

Questions

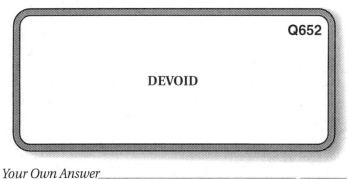

Q652

DEVOID

*Your Own Answer*_____

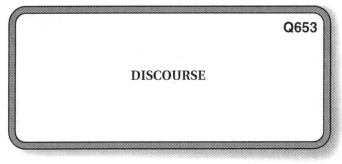

Q653

DISCOURSE

*Your Own Answer*_____

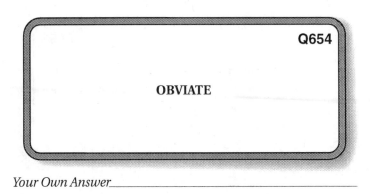

Q654

OBVIATE

*Your Own Answer*_____

Correct Answers

A652

adj.—lacking; empty

The interplanetary probe indicated that the planet was **devoid** of any atmosphere.

A653

v.—to converse; to communicate in an orderly fashion

The interviewee **discoursed** so fluently that she was hired on the spot.

A654

v.—to make unnecessary

The invention of cars has **obviated** the use of the horse and carriage.

Questions

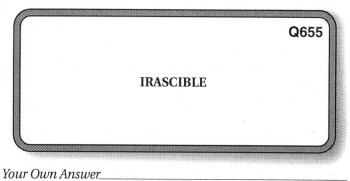

Q655

IRASCIBLE

*Your Own Answer*_____

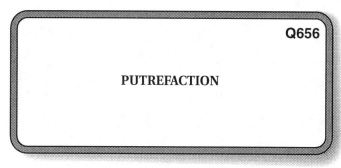

Q656

PUTREFACTION

*Your Own Answer*_____

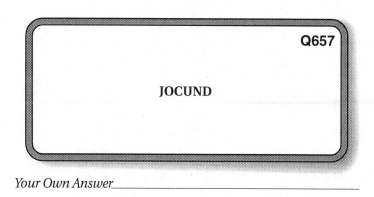

Q657

JOCUND

*Your Own Answer*_____

Correct Answers

A655

adj.—prone to anger

The **irascible** teenager was known to cause fights when upset.

A656

n.—a mass of decomposed organic matter

The jack-o-lantern was reduced to **putrefaction** by Thanksgiving.

A657

adj.—happy; cheerful

The **jocund** atmosphere was due to the team's victory in the playoffs.

Questions

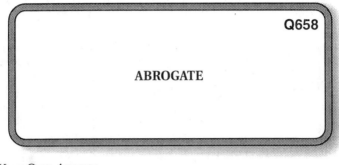

Q658

ABROGATE

*Your Own Answer*_____

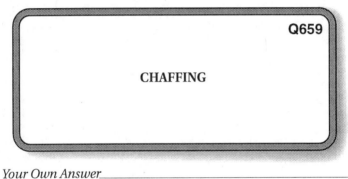

Q659

CHAFFING

*Your Own Answer*_____

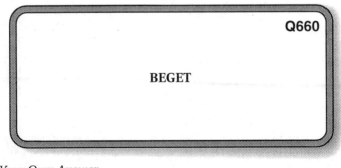

Q660

BEGET

*Your Own Answer*_____

Correct Answers

v.—to cancel by authority
The judge said he could not **abrogate** the law.

n.—banter; teasing
The king was used to his jester's good-natured **chaffing**.

v.—to bring into being
The king wished to **beget** a new heir.

Questions

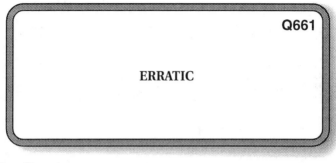

Q661

ERRATIC

*Your Own Answer*_____

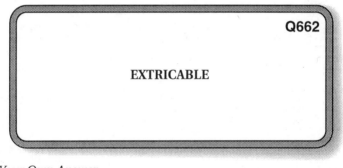

Q662

EXTRICABLE

*Your Own Answer*_____

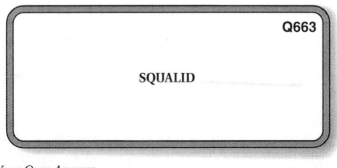

Q663

SQUALID

*Your Own Answer*_____

Correct Answers

A661

adj.—unpredictable; strange
The kitten's **erratic** behavior was attributed to the owner's cruel method of disciplining his pet.

A662

adj.—capable of being disentangled or disengaged
She was glad to be **extricable** from the dangerous situation.

A663

adj.—filthy; wretched (from squalor)
The lack of sanitation piping caused **squalid** conditions.

Questions

Q664

LAMBENT

*Your Own Answer*_____

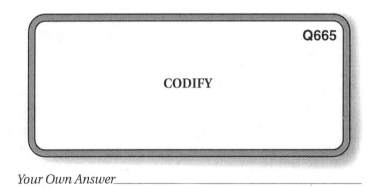

Q665

CODIFY

*Your Own Answer*_____

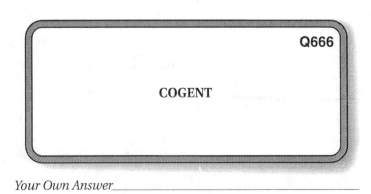

Q666

COGENT

*Your Own Answer*_____

Correct Answers

A664

adj.—traveling gently over surface; flickering

The **lambent** flame lit the dark room as the breeze wafted in.

A665

v.—to organize laws or rules into a systematic collection

The laws were **codified** by those whom they affected.

A666

adj.—to the point; clear; convincing in its clarity and presentation

The lawyer makes compelling and **cogent** presentations, which evidently help him win 96 percent of his cases.

Questions

Q667

DISPARAGE

*Your Own Answer*_____

Q668

MITIGATE

*Your Own Answer*_____

Q669

LECHEROUS

*Your Own Answer*_____

Correct Answers

A667

v.—to discredit

The lawyer will attempt to **disparage** the testimony of the witness.

A668

v.—to make less severe

The lawyer will attempt to **mitigate** the sentence.

A669

adj.—characterized by lewdness

The **lecherous** man lurked on the corner.

Questions

Q670

LIGNEOUS

*Your Own Answer*_____

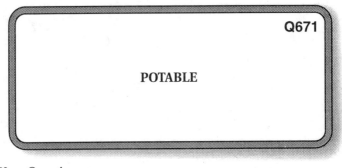

Q671

POTABLE

*Your Own Answer*_____

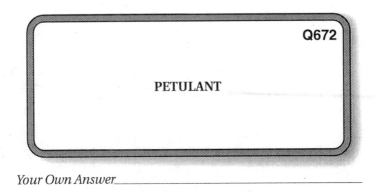

Q672

PETULANT

*Your Own Answer*_____

Correct Answers

adj.—having the composition of wood

The **ligneous** material was maple.

adj.—drinkable

The liquid was not **potable**, but poisonous.

adj.—peevish; cranky; irritable

The long illness put the boy in a **petulant** mood.

Questions

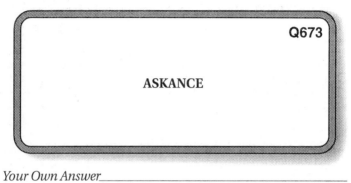

Q673

ASKANCE

*Your Own Answer*_____

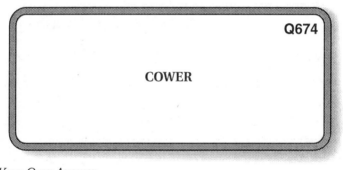

Q674

COWER

*Your Own Answer*_____

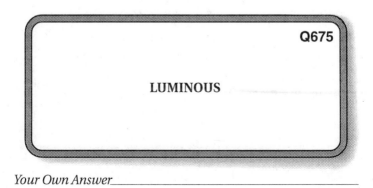

Q675

LUMINOUS

*Your Own Answer*_____

Correct Answers

A673

adv.—a sideways glance of disapproval

The look **askance** proved the guard suspected some wrongdoing.

A674

v.—to huddle and tremble

The lost dog **cowered** near the tree.

A675

adj.—emitting light; shining; also enlightened or intelligent

The **luminous** quality of the precious stone made it look like a fallen star.

Questions

Q676

OBFUSCATE

*Your Own Answer*_____

_____

Q677

PARADIGM

*Your Own Answer*_____

_____

Q678

MACULATE

*Your Own Answer*_____

_____

Correct Answers

v.—to darken; to confuse; to bewilder

The professor **obfuscated** the theory with extraneous information, instead of making it clearer to his students.

n.—a model; a prototype; a pattern

The machine could no longer be produced after the **paradigm** was destroyed.

adj.—spotted; blotched; defiled; impure (opposite: immaculate)

The **maculate** furniture was covered in what appeared to be food stains.

Questions

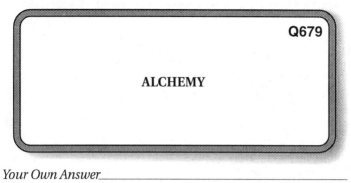

Q679

ALCHEMY

*Your Own Answer*_____

_____

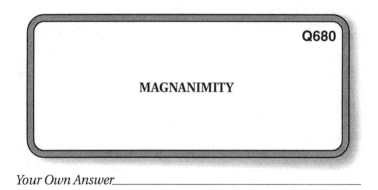

Q680

MAGNANIMITY

*Your Own Answer*_____

_____

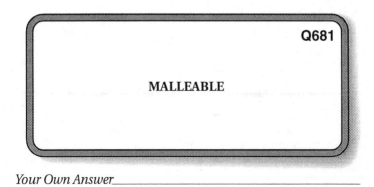

Q681

MALLEABLE

*Your Own Answer*_____

_____

Correct Answers

A679

n.—any magical power or process of transmuting

The medieval sorcerer used **alchemy** to change the dust into poison.

A680

n.—a quality of nobleness of mind, disdaining meanness or revenge

The **magnanimity** of the professor overcame the rage of the student.

A681

adj.—easy to shape or bend; pliable

The **malleable** material was formed into a "U" shape.

Questions

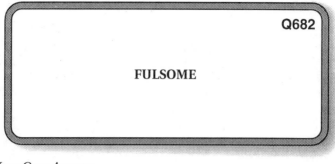

Q682

FULSOME

*Your Own Answer*_____

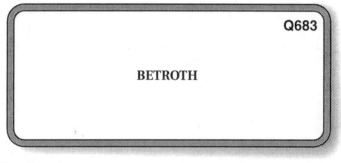

Q683

BETROTH

*Your Own Answer*_____

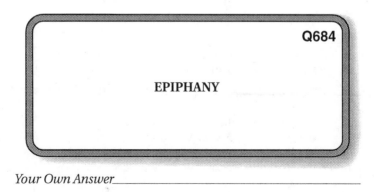

Q684

EPIPHANY

*Your Own Answer*_____

Correct Answers

A682

adj.—disgusting due to excess

The man became obese when he indulged in **fulsome** eating.

A683

v.—to promise or pledge in marriage

The man **betrothed** his daughter to the prince.

A684

n.—a sudden, intuitive insight into reality or the essential meaning of something, usually initiated by simple common experience (often in a literary work describing this experience)

The passage described the boy's **epiphany** about the meaning of life after seeing the deer die.

Questions

Q685

DISSEMBLE

*Your Own Answer*_____

Q686

DEFUNCT

*Your Own Answer*_____

Q687

MALEVOLENT

*Your Own Answer*_____

Correct Answers

A685

v.—to pretend; to feign; to conceal by pretense

The man **dissembled** his assets shamelessly to avoid paying alimony.

A686

adj.—no longer living or existing

The man lost a large sum of money when the company went **defunct**.

A687

adj.—wishing evil (opposite: benevolent)

The man threatened his opponent with threats and **malevolent** words.

Questions

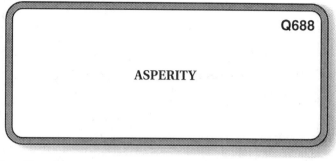

Q688

ASPERITY

*Your Own Answer*_____

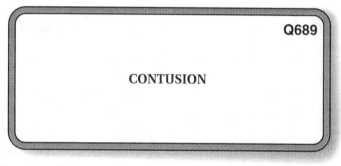

Q689

CONTUSION

*Your Own Answer*_____

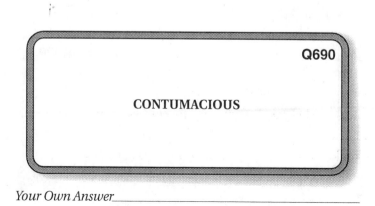

Q690

CONTUMACIOUS

*Your Own Answer*_____

Correct Answers

n.—harshness

The man used **asperity** to frighten the girl out of going.

n.—a bruise; an injury in which the skin is not broken

The man was fortunate to receive only **contusions** from the crash.

adj.—resisting authority

The man was put in jail for **contumacious** actions.

Questions

Q691

TACITURN

*Your Own Answer*_____

Q692

DESCANT

*Your Own Answer*_____

Q693

OBSEQUIOUS

*Your Own Answer*_____

Correct Answers

A691

adj.—inclined to silence; speaking little; dour; stern

The man was so **taciturn** that his presence was forgotten.

A692

v.—to talk or write at length

The man will **descant** on the subject if you give him too much speaking time.

A693

adj.—servilely attentive; fawning

The man's **obsequious** behavior made his attraction to the woman evident.

Questions

Q694

AVARICE

*Your Own Answer*_____

Q695

REPREHENSIBLE

*Your Own Answer*_____

Q696

IMMUTABLE

*Your Own Answer*_____

Correct Answers

A694

n.—inordinate desire for gaining and possessing wealth

The man's **avarice** kept him at work through the evenings and weekends so he would have more money to buy luxuries.

A695

adj.—deserving a reprimand

The man's failure to remember the meeting was totally **reprehensible**.

A696

adj.—never varying

The man's **immutable** schedule soon became boring.

Questions

Q697

LUGUBRIOUS

*Your Own Answer*_____

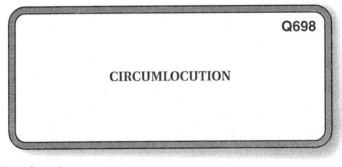

Q698

CIRCUMLOCUTION

*Your Own Answer*_____

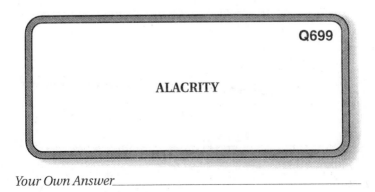

Q699

ALACRITY

*Your Own Answer*_____

Correct Answers

A697

adj.—full of sorrow; mournful

The man's **lugubrious** heart kept him from enjoying the special occasion.

A698

n.—a roundabout or indirect way of speaking; not to the point

The man's speech contained so much **circumlocution** that I was unsure of the point he was trying to make.

A699

n.—eager readiness or speed

The manager was so impressed by the worker's **alacrity** that he suggested a promotion.

Questions

Q700

MARAUDER

*Your Own Answer*_____

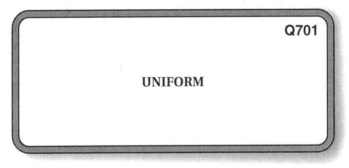

Q701

UNIFORM

*Your Own Answer*_____

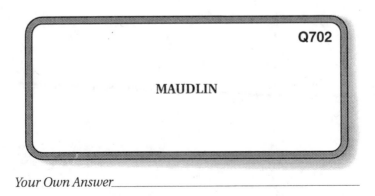

Q702

MAUDLIN

*Your Own Answer*_____

Correct Answers

A700

n.—plunderer or raider

The **marauder** had been traveling for two months searching for the large stash.

A701

adj.—never changing; always with the same standard

The products were **uniform** in quality.

A702

adj.—foolishly and tearfully sentimental

The **maudlin** affair consisted of three speeches in honor of the benefactor.

Questions

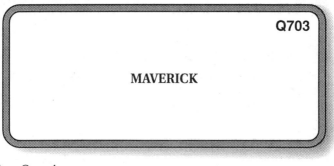

Q703

MAVERICK

*Your Own Answer*_____

_____

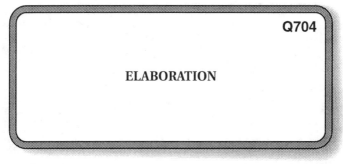

Q704

ELABORATION

*Your Own Answer*_____

_____

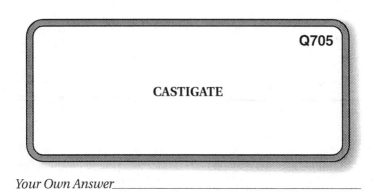

Q705

CASTIGATE

*Your Own Answer*_____

_____

Correct Answers

n.—a person who does not conform to the norm

The **maverick** drove a large truck while others were purchasing compact cars.

n.—act of clarifying; adding details

The mayor called for an **elaboration** on the ordinance's first draft.

v.—to punish through public criticism

The mayor **castigated** the police chief for the rash of robberies.

Questions

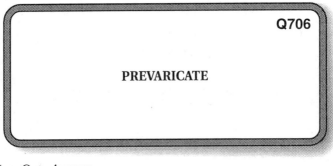

Q706

PREVARICATE

*Your Own Answer*_____

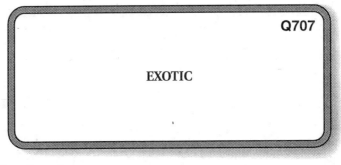

Q707

EXOTIC

*Your Own Answer*_____

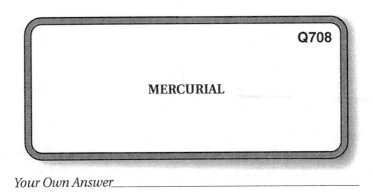

Q708

MERCURIAL

*Your Own Answer*_____

Correct Answers

A706

v.—to speak equivocally or evasively; to lie

The mayor's desperate attempt to **prevaricate** about the scandal was transparent to the voters.

A707

adj.—unusual; striking

The menu of authentic Turkish cuisine seemed **exotic** to them, considering they were only accustomed to American food.

A708

adj.—quick; changeable; fickle

The **mercurial** youth changed outfits six times before deciding what to wear.

Questions

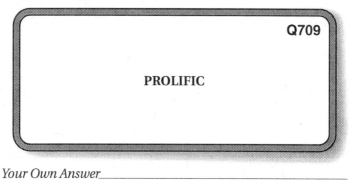

Q709

PROLIFIC

*Your Own Answer*_____

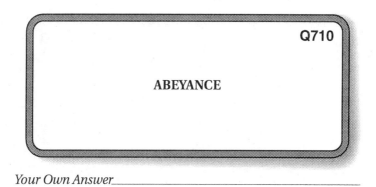

Q710

ABEYANCE

*Your Own Answer*_____

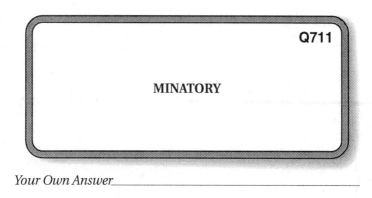

Q711

MINATORY

*Your Own Answer*_____

Correct Answers

A709

adj.—fruitful

The merger resulted in a **prolific** business which became an asset to the community.

A710

n.—a state of temporary suspension of activity

The power failure held the town's activities in **abeyance**.

A711

adj.—threatening

The **minatory** stance of the dog warned the thief of an attack.

Questions

Q712

INCORRIGIBLE

*Your Own Answer*_____

Q713

PRESCIENCE

*Your Own Answer*_____

Q714

INCESSANT

*Your Own Answer*_____

Correct Answers

A712

adj.—not capable of correction or improvement

The mischievous boy was an **incorrigible** practical joker.

A713

n.—knowing about something before it happens

The morning of the big game I had a **prescience** that we would win.

A714

adj.—constant and unending

The mother gave in to the child after her **incessant** crying.

Questions

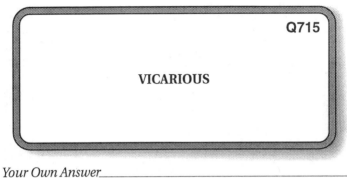

Q715

VICARIOUS

*Your Own Answer*_____

_____

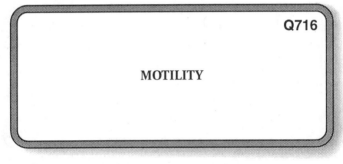

Q716

MOTILITY

*Your Own Answer*_____

_____

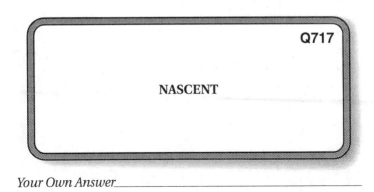

Q717

NASCENT

*Your Own Answer*_____

_____

Correct Answers

A715

adj.—done or sacrificed for others

The father would have endured **vicarious** punishment for his son if the judge imposed it.

A716

n.—spontaneous motion

The **motility** of the car caused the driver to lunge for the brake.

A717

adj.—starting to grow or develop

The **nascent** rage of in-line skating began on the West Coast.

Questions

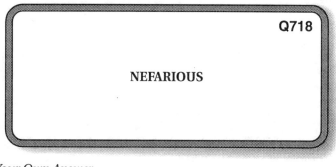

Q718

NEFARIOUS

*Your Own Answer*_____

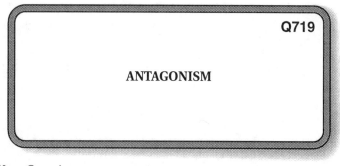

Q719

ANTAGONISM

*Your Own Answer*_____

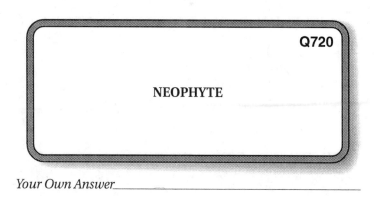

Q720

NEOPHYTE

*Your Own Answer*_____

Correct Answers

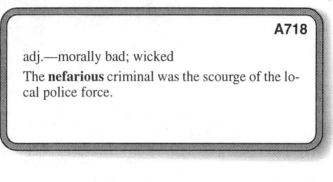

A718

adj.—morally bad; wicked

The **nefarious** criminal was the scourge of the local police force.

A719

n.—hostility; opposition

The neighbor's **antagonism** was fueled by a simple misunderstanding.

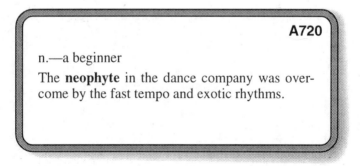

A720

n.—a beginner

The **neophyte** in the dance company was overcome by the fast tempo and exotic rhythms.

Questions

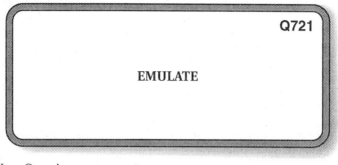

Q721

EMULATE

*Your Own Answer*_____

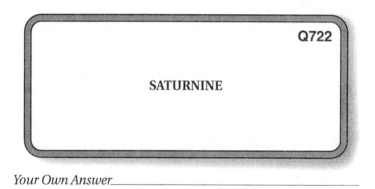

Q722

SATURNINE

*Your Own Answer*_____

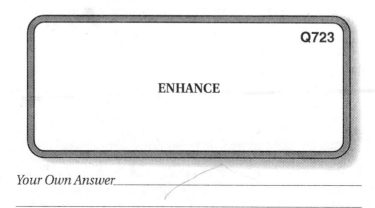

Q723

ENHANCE

*Your Own Answer*_____

Correct Answers

A721

v.—to try to equal or surpass

The new teacher was hoping to **emulate** her mentor.

A722

adj.—gloomy; sluggish

The neverending rain put everyone in a **saturnine** mood.

A723

v.—to improve; to compliment; to make more attractive

The new fuel **enhanced** the performance of the rocket's engines.

Questions

Q724

COMMODIOUS

*Your Own Answer*_____

_____

Q725

PALATIAL

*Your Own Answer*_____

_____

Q726

FACILITATE

*Your Own Answer*_____

_____

Correct Answers

A724

adj.—spacious and convenient; roomy

The new home was so **commodious** that many new pieces of furniture needed to be purchased.

A725

adj.—large and ornate; like a palace

The new **palatial** home contained two pools and an indoor track for jogging.

A726

v.—to make easier; to simplify

The new ramp by the door's entrance **facilitated** access to the building for those in wheelchairs.

Questions

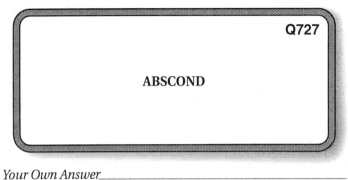

Q727

ABSCOND

*Your Own Answer*_____

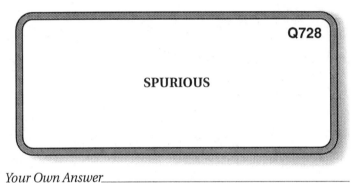

Q728

SPURIOUS

*Your Own Answer*_____

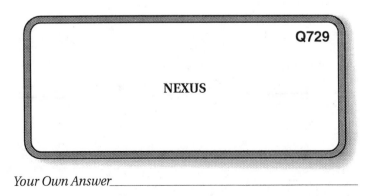

Q729

NEXUS

*Your Own Answer*_____

Correct Answers

A727

v.—to go away hastily or secretly; to hide

The newlyweds **absconded** from the reception to jet off on their honeymoon.

A728

adj.—not genuine; false; bogus

The newspaper was notorious for **spurious** information.

A729

n.—a connection

The **nexus** between the shuttle and the space station was successful.

Questions

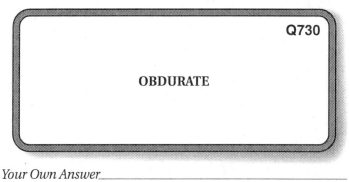

Q730

OBDURATE

*Your Own Answer*_____

_____

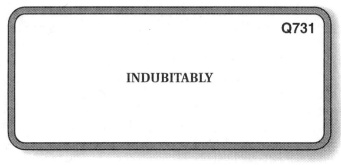

Q731

INDUBITABLY

*Your Own Answer*_____

_____

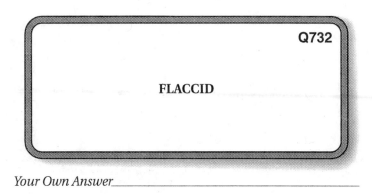

Q732

FLACCID

*Your Own Answer*_____

_____

Correct Answers

A730

adj.—stubborn
The **obdurate** child refused to go to school.

A731

adv.—unquestionably; surely
The officer was **indubitably** the best candidate for captain.

A732

adj.—lacking firmness; limp
The old dog's **flaccid** tail refused to wag.

Questions

Q733

HALCYON

Your Own Answer_____

Q734

FLINCH

Your Own Answer_____

Q735

OLIGARCHY

Your Own Answer_____

Correct Answers

adj.—tranquil; happy

The old man fondly remembered his **halcyon** days growing up on the farm.

v.—to wince; to drawback; to retreat

The older brother made his younger sister **flinch** when he jokingly tried to punch her arm.

n.—form of government in which the supreme power is placed in the hands of a small, exclusive group

The **oligarchy** took control after the king was overthrown.

Questions

Q736

PROSAIC

*Your Own Answer*_____

Q737

PRECEPT

*Your Own Answer*_____

Q738

DEPRECATE

*Your Own Answer*_____

Correct Answers

A736

adj.—ordinary and dull

The only entertainment would be a **prosaic** game of cards.

A737

n.—a rule or direction of moral conduct

The organization believed its members should abide by certain **precepts**.

A738

v.—to express disapproval of; to protest against

The organization will **deprecate** the opening of the sewage plant.

Questions

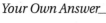

OSTENSIBLE

*Your Own Answer*_____

PARSIMONIOUS

*Your Own Answer*_____

VIABLE

*Your Own Answer*_____

Correct Answers

adj.—apparent
The **ostensible** reason for choosing the girl was for her beauty.

adj.—very frugal; unwilling to spend
The owner was so **parsimonious** he refused to purchase new curtains when the old ones fell off the window.

adj.—able to live or grow; possible
The package said the plant was **viable** in hot climates.

Questions

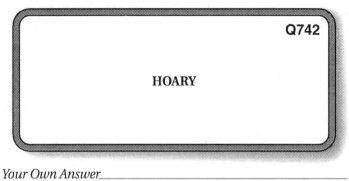

Q742

HOARY

*Your Own Answer*_____

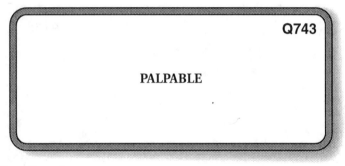

Q743

PALPABLE

*Your Own Answer*_____

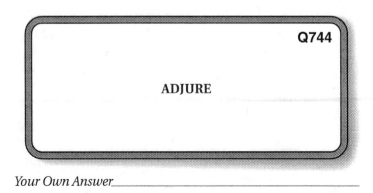

Q744

ADJURE

*Your Own Answer*_____

Correct Answers

A742

adj.—whitened by age

The paint had a **hoary** appearance, as if it were applied decades ago.

A743

adj.—touchable; clear, obvious

The **palpable** decision was to discontinue the use of drugs.

A744

v.—to solemnly order

The panel was **adjured** by the judge to make its decision based on the law.

Questions

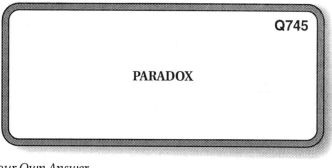

Q745

PARADOX

*Your Own Answer*_____

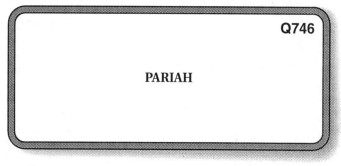

Q746

PARIAH

*Your Own Answer*_____

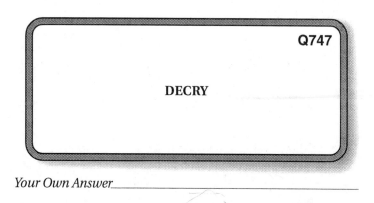

Q747

DECRY

*Your Own Answer*_____

Correct Answers

A745

n.—a tenet seemingly contradictory or false, but actually true

The **paradox** seemed so unlikely though it was true.

A746

n.—an outcast

The **pariah** of the group sat by himself under the tree.

A747

v.—to denounce or condemn openly

The pastor **decried** all forms of discrimination against any minority group.

Questions

ADVERSARY

*Your Own Answer*_____

PELLUCID

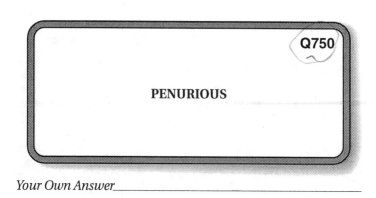

*Your Own Answer*_____

PENURIOUS

*Your Own Answer*_____

Correct Answers

A748

n.—an enemy; a foe

The peace treaty united two countries that had been great **adversaries**.

A749

adj.—transparent

The **pellucid** material was not an adequate shield from the sun.

A750

adj.—stingy; miserly

The **penurious** man had millions of dollars, but lived in a cottage to save money.

Questions

morally lacking restrain

LICENTIOUS

*Your Own Answer*_____

stimulate by electric

GALVANIZE shock.

*Your Own Answer*_____

eternal
↓ ↓ damnation.

PERDITION

*Your Own Answer*_____

Correct Answers

A751

adj.—morally lacking in restraint

The people of Sodom and Gomorrah were infamous for their **licentious** lifestyle.

A752

v.—to stimulate as if by electric shock; to startle; to excite

The pep rally will **galvanize** the team.

A753

n.—eternal damnation of the soul

The woman attended church every Sunday for fear of **perdition**.

Questions

Q754

causing
↓ dest. or death

PERNICIOUS

*Your Own Answer*_____

Q755

Rough or disturb
↓

FRET

✓

*Your Own Answer*_____

Q756

Plundering.
↓ or laying waste.

DEPREDATION

*Your Own Answer*_____

Correct Answers

A754

adj.—causing destruction or death
The **pernicious** fire engulfed four blocks of homes.

A755

v.—to make rough or disturb
The pet will **fret** the floor if he continues to scratch.

A756

n.—a plundering or laying waste
The pharaoh's once rich tomb was empty after centuries of **depredation** from grave robbers.

Questions

Q757

provide
ENDUE

*Your Own Answer*_____

Q758

sluggish, dull)
PHLEGMATIC

*Your Own Answer*_____

Q759

undisturbed, calm
PLACID

*Your Own Answer*_____

Correct Answers

A757

v.—to provide
The philanthropist agreed to **endue** the hospital with the necessary funding.

A758

adj.—sluggish and dull
The **phlegmatic** child rarely went outside to play.

A759

adj.—undisturbed and calm
The **placid** lake's water was completely motion-less.

Questions

Shave off

Tear down or obliterate

RAZE

*Your Own Answer*_____

witty poem

EPIGRAM

*Your Own Answer*_____

POLEMIC controversial

*Your Own Answer*_____

Correct Answers

A760

v.—to scrape or shave off; to obliterate or tear down completely

The plow will **raze** the ice from the road surface.

A761

n.—a witty or satirical poem or statement

The poet wrote an **epigram** about the upcoming election.

A762

adj.—controversial

The **polemic** decision caused a stir in the community.

Questions

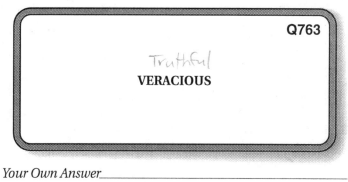

Q763

Truthful
VERACIOUS

Your Own Answer_____

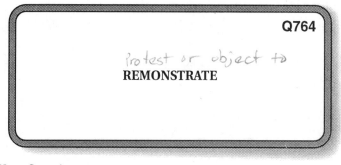

Q764

Protest or object to
REMONSTRATE

Your Own Answer_____

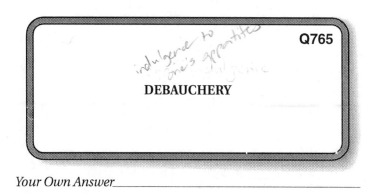

Q765

indulgence to
one's appetites

DEBAUCHERY

Your Own Answer_____

Correct Answers

A763

adj.—truthful
The politician presented a **veracious** and dependable image.

A764

v.—to protest or object to
The population will **remonstrate** against the new taxes.

A765

n.—indulgence in one's appetites
The preacher decried **debauchery** and urged charity.

Questions

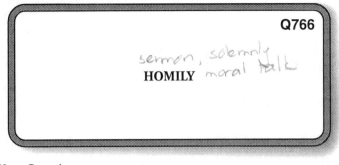

Q766

sermon, solemnly

HOMILY moral talk

*Your Own Answer*_____

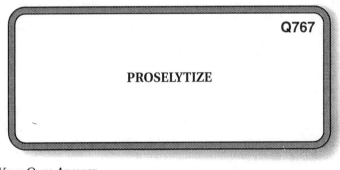

Q767

PROSELYTIZE

*Your Own Answer*_____

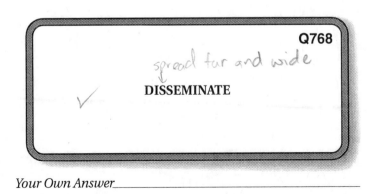

Q768

spread far and wide

DISSEMINATE

*Your Own Answer*_____

Correct Answers

A766

n.—solemn moral talk; sermon

The preacher gave a moving **homily** to the gathered crowd.

A767

v.—to try to convert a person from one belief or religion to another

The preacher often attempts to **proselytize** wayward travelers.

A768

v.—to spread far and wide

The preacher traveled across the country to **disseminate** his message.

Questions

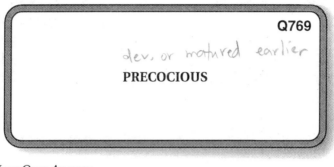

Q769

dev, or matured earlier

PRECOCIOUS

*Your Own Answer*_____

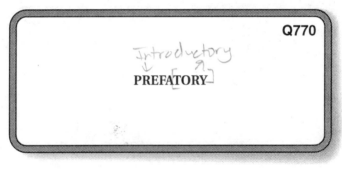

Q770

Introductory

PREFATORY

*Your Own Answer*_____

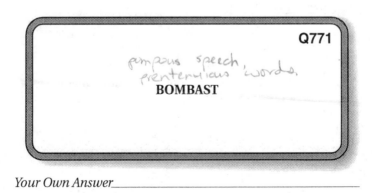

Q771

pompous speech, pretentious words.

BOMBAST

*Your Own Answer*_____

Correct Answers

A769

adj.—developed or matured earlier than usual

The **precocious** eight-year-old wanted to read the romance novel.

A770

adj.—introductory

The **prefatory** comments informed the audience of what was to come.

A771

n.—pompous speech; pretentious words

The presenter ended his **bombast** with a prediction of his future success.

Questions

Q772

line of descent

PROGENY

✓

Your Own Answer_____

Q773

praise in
excess

ADULATION

Your Own Answer_____

Q774

one who commits
to a crime

MALEFACTOR

Your Own Answer_____

Correct Answers

A772

n.—line of descent
The princes were the **progeny** of royalty.

A773

n.—praise in excess
The princess attracted **adulation** like few other people in recent history.

A774

n.—one who commits a crime
The prison contains **malefactors** of all ages.

Questions

Q775

PRISTINE

*Your Own Answer*_____

_____

Q776

HYPOTHETICAL

*Your Own Answer*_____

_____

Q777

PROTOCOL

*Your Own Answer*_____

_____

Correct Answers

A775

adj.—primitive; pure; uncorrupted

The **pristine** lake had not been marred by pollution.

A776

adj.—assumed; uncertain

The professor was good at using **hypothetical** situations to illustrate complicated theories.

A777

n.—an original draft or record of a document

The **protocol** was given to the president once it was completed.

Questions

Q778

PUERILE

*Your Own Answer*_____

Q779

SUFFUSE

*Your Own Answer*_____

Q780

FERMENT

*Your Own Answer*_____

Correct Answers

A778

adj.—childlike; silly

The **puerile** actions of the man caused him to lose his promotion.

A779

v.—to overspread

The room was **suffused** with light from the bay window.

A780

v.—to excite or agitate

The rally cry was meant to **ferment** and confuse the opponent.

Questions

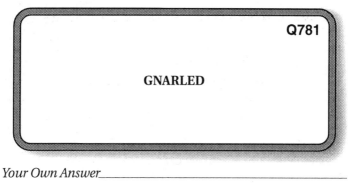

Q781

GNARLED

*Your Own Answer*_____

_____

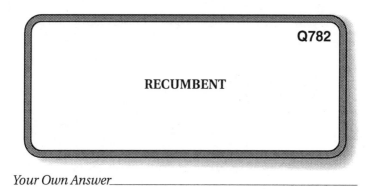

Q782

RECUMBENT

*Your Own Answer*_____

_____

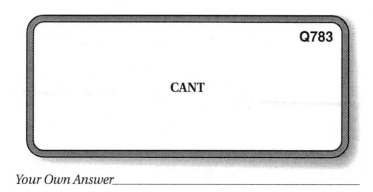

Q783

CANT

*Your Own Answer*_____

_____

Correct Answers

A781

adj.—full of knots; twisted

The raven perched in the **gnarled** branches of the ancient tree.

A782

adj.—resting

The **recumbent** puppy stirred.

A783

n.—insincere or hypocritical statements of high ideal; the jargon of a particular group or occupation

The doctor's **cant** was meant only for his associates.

Questions

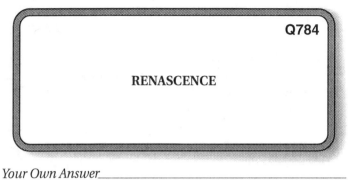

Q784

RENASCENCE

*Your Own Answer*_____

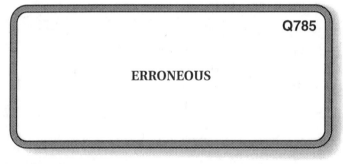

Q785

ERRONEOUS

*Your Own Answer*_____

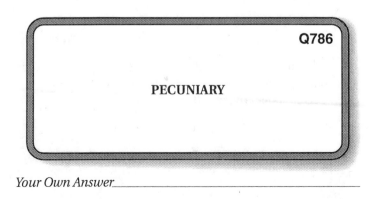

Q786

PECUNIARY

*Your Own Answer*_____

Correct Answers

A784

n.—a new life; rebirth

The **renascence** of the band resulted in a new recording contract.

A785

adj.—untrue; inaccurate; not correct

The reporter's **erroneous** story was corrected by a new article that stated the truth.

A786

adj.—pertaining to money

The retiring employee was delighted when he received a **pecuniary** gift.

Questions

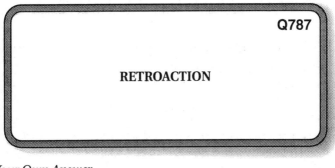

Q787

RETROACTION

*Your Own Answer*_____

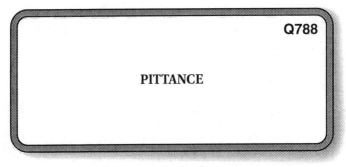

Q788

PITTANCE

*Your Own Answer*_____

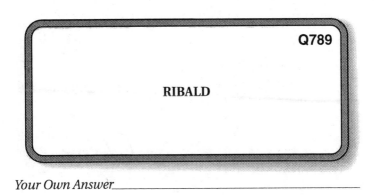

Q789

RIBALD

*Your Own Answer*_____

Correct Answers

n.—a reverse action

Just to make him mad, she performed the **retro-action** to every action he performed.

n.—a small amount

The reward money was only a **pittance** compared to the money lost.

adj.—characterized by vulgar joking

The **ribald** story proved an embarrassment to its audience.

Questions

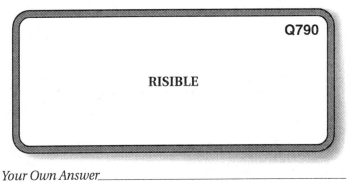

Q790

RISIBLE

*Your Own Answer*_____

Q791

HAMPER

*Your Own Answer*_____

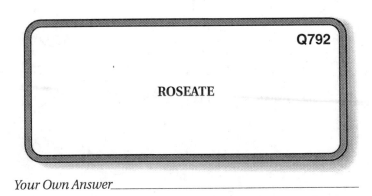

Q792

ROSEATE

*Your Own Answer*_____

Correct Answers

adj.—amusing
The **risible** speech made the audience chuckle.

v.—interfere with; to hinder
The road block **hampered** their progress, but luckily, they knew the back roads well.

adj.—rose-colored
The **roseate** sunset faded into the sky.

Questions

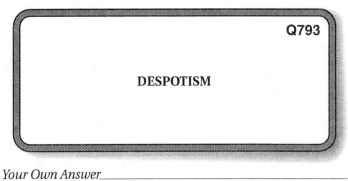

Q793

DESPOTISM

*Your Own Answer*_____

_____

Q794

GLIB

*Your Own Answer*_____

_____

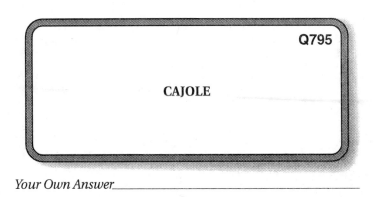

Q795

CAJOLE

*Your Own Answer*_____

_____

Correct Answers

A793

n.—tyranny; absolute power or influence

The ruler's **despotism** went uncontested for 30 years.

A794

adj.—smooth and slippery; speaking or spoken in a smooth manner

The salesman was so **glib** that the customers failed to notice the defects in the stereo.

A795

v.—to use flattery and insincere talk to coax

The salesman will **cajole** the couple into buying the stereo.

Questions

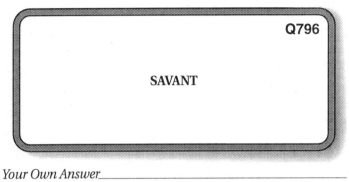

Q796

SAVANT

*Your Own Answer*_____

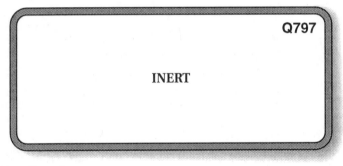

Q797

INERT

*Your Own Answer*_____

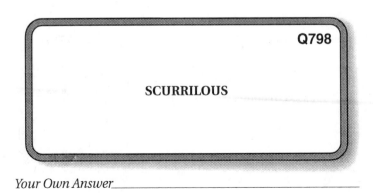

Q798

SCURRILOUS

*Your Own Answer*_____

Correct Answers

A796

n.—one who is learned; a scholar
The **savant** accepted his award of excellence.

A797

adj.—not reacting chemically; inactive
The scientist was unable to repeat the experiment
with only **inert** chemicals.

A798

adj.—using vulgarity
The **scurrilous** language made the mother twinge.

Questions

Q799

SHODDY

*Your Own Answer*_____

_____

Q800

TAWDRY

*Your Own Answer*_____

_____

Q801

UNOBTRUSIVE

*Your Own Answer*_____

_____

Correct Answers

A799

adj.—of inferior quality

The **shoddy** homes were blown over in the storm.

A800

adj.—tastelessly ornamented

The costume shop was full of **tawdry** jewelry.

A801

adj.—out of the way; remaining quietly in the background

The shy man found an **unobtrusive** seat in the far corner of the room.

Questions

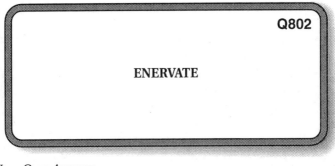

Q802

ENERVATE

*Your Own Answer*_____

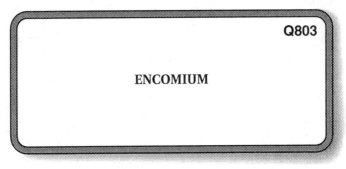

Q803

ENCOMIUM

*Your Own Answer*_____

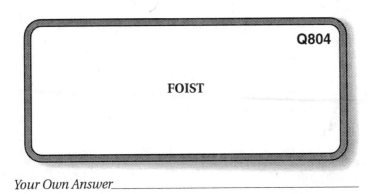

Q804

FOIST

*Your Own Answer*_____

Correct Answers

A802

v.—to weaken; to deprive of nerve or strength

The sickness **enervates** its victims until they can no longer get out of bed.

A803

n.—a formal expression of high praise

The sitcom actress gave her co-stars a long **encomium** as she accepted her Emmy.

A804

v.—to falsely identify as real

The smuggler tried to **foist** the cut glass as a priceless gem.

Questions

DELIQUESCE

*Your Own Answer*_____

UNCOUTH

*Your Own Answer*_____

MALINGER

*Your Own Answer*_____

Correct Answers

A805

v.—to melt away
The snow **deliquesced** when the temperature rose.

A806

adj.—uncultured; crude
The social club would not accept an **uncouth** individual.

A807

v.—to fake illness in order to escape duty
The soldier will **malinger** to avoid fighting.

Questions

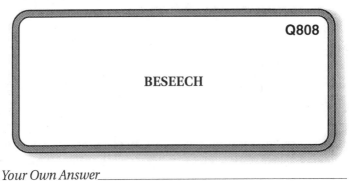

Q808

BESEECH

*Your Own Answer*_____

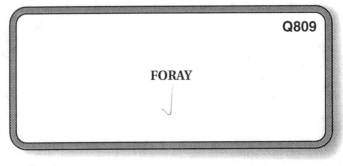

Q809

FORAY

*Your Own Answer*_____

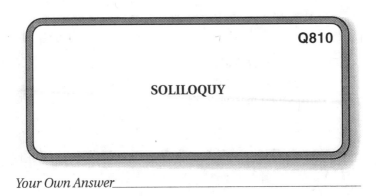

Q810

SOLILOQUY

*Your Own Answer*_____

Correct Answers

v.—to ask earnestly
The soldiers **beseeched** the civilians for help.

v.—to raid for spoils; to plunder
The soldiers were told not to **foray** the town.

n.—the act of speaking to oneself
The **soliloquy** by the man, standing alone on the cliff, sent a message of regret.

Questions

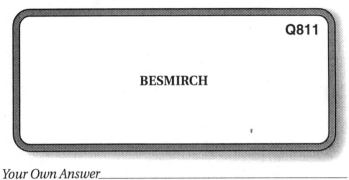

Q811

BESMIRCH

*Your Own Answer*_____

Q812

ELOQUENCE

*Your Own Answer*_____

Q813

SPELUNKER

*Your Own Answer*_____

Correct Answers

A811

v.—to dirty or discolor

The soot from the chimney will **besmirch** the clean curtains.

A812

n.—the ability to speak well

She spoke with **eloquence**, keeping the crowd attentive and pleased.

A813

n.—one who explores and studies caves

The **spelunker** made a startling discovery in the old mine.

Questions

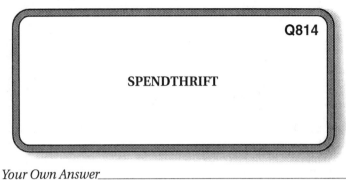

Q814

SPENDTHRIFT

*Your Own Answer*_____

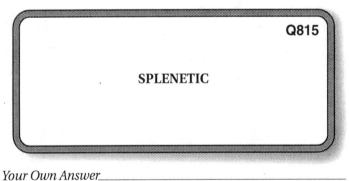

Q815

SPLENETIC

*Your Own Answer*_____

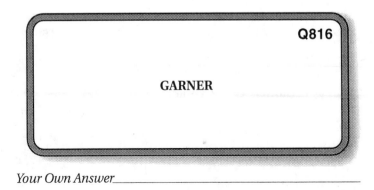

Q816

GARNER

*Your Own Answer*_____

Correct Answers

A814

n.—a person who spends money extravagantly

The **spendthrift** bought two new necklaces and three pairs of shoes.

A815

adj.—irritable and spiteful

The **splenetic** warriors advanced with no thought of what they were destroying.

A816

v.—to gather up and store; to collect

The squirrels **garnered** nuts for the winter.

Questions

LOQUACIOUS

*Your Own Answer*_____

EON

*Your Own Answer*_____

STATIC

*Your Own Answer*_____

Correct Answers

A817

adj.—very talkative

The staff knew the meeting would be long because the administrator was in a **loquacious** mood.

A818

n.—an indefinitely long period of time

The star may have existed for **eons**.

A819

adj.—to remain still, with no movement

The **static** water of the lake reflected the image of the trees.

Questions

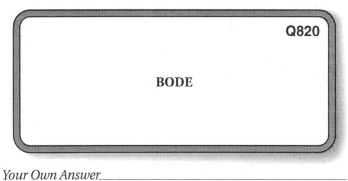

Q820

BODE

*Your Own Answer*_____

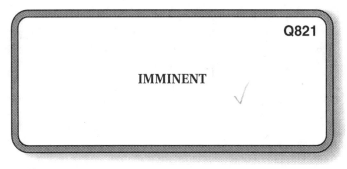

Q821

IMMINENT

*Your Own Answer*_____

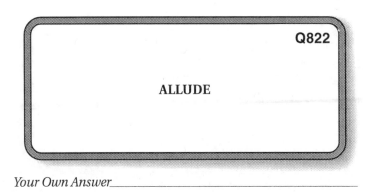

Q822

ALLUDE

*Your Own Answer*_____

Correct Answers

v.—to foretell something
The storm **bode** that we would not reach our destination.

adj.—likely to happen without delay
The storm clouds warned of the **imminent** downpour.

v.—to refer indirectly to something
The story **alludes** to part of the author's life.

Questions

CONTRAVENE

*Your Own Answer*_____

BALEFUL

*Your Own Answer*_____

STRIATED

*Your Own Answer*_____

Correct Answers

A823

v.—to act contrary to; to oppose or contradict

The story of the accused **contravened** the story of the witness.

A824

adj.—harmful

The strange liquid could be **baleful** if ingested.

A825

adj.—having lines or grooves

The **striated** lane was closed to traffic.

Questions

INNUENDO

*Your Own Answer*_____

OSTRACIZE

*Your Own Answer*_____

RECONDITE

*Your Own Answer*_____

Correct Answers

A826

n.—an indirect remark, usually derogatory

The student made an **innuendo** referring to the professor.

A827

v.—to exclude

The students tend to **ostracize** the children they dislike from their games.

A828

adj.—hard to understand; concealed

The students were dumbfounded by the **recondite** topic.

Questions

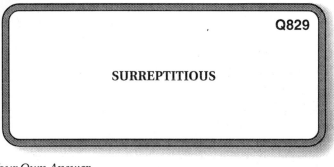

Q829

SURREPTITIOUS

*Your Own Answer*_____

_____

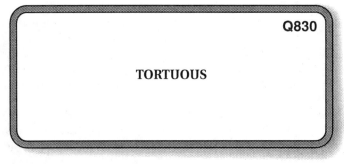

Q830

TORTUOUS

*Your Own Answer*_____

_____

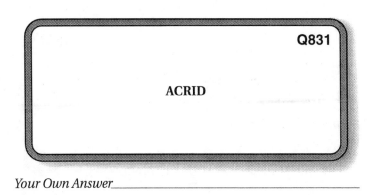

Q831

ACRID

*Your Own Answer*_____

_____

Correct Answers

A829

adj.—done secretly

The **surreptitious** maneuvers gave the advancing army an advantage.

A830

adj.—full of twists and turns; not straightforward; possibly deceitful

The suspect confessed after the **tortuous** questioning by the captain.

A831

adj.—sharp or biting to the taste or smell; irritating to the eyes, nose

The swamp is **acrid** due to its proximity to the sewer discharge.

Questions

Q832

LEVEE

*Your Own Answer*_____

_____

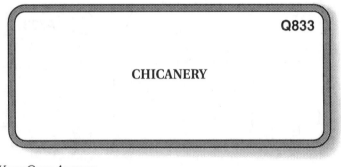

Q833

CHICANERY

*Your Own Answer*_____

_____

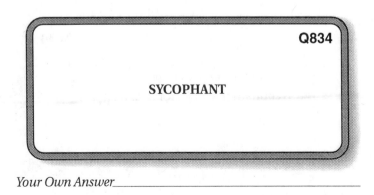

Q834

SYCOPHANT

*Your Own Answer*_____

_____

Correct Answers

A832

n.—a landing on the edge of a river or field
The swimmer came ashore on the **levee**.

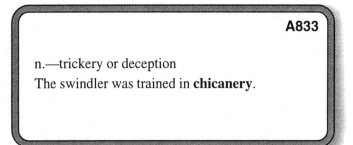

A833

n.—trickery or deception
The swindler was trained in **chicanery**.

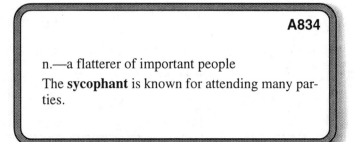

A834

n.—a flatterer of important people
The **sycophant** is known for attending many parties.

Questions

SYLLOGISM

*Your Own Answer*_____

_____

OSSIFY

*Your Own Answer*_____

_____

VOLUBLE

*Your Own Answer*_____

_____

Correct Answers

A835

n.—reasoning from the general to the particular
The **syllogism** went from fish to guppies.

A836

v.—to turn to bone; to harden like bone
The tablet will **ossify** when left in the sun.

A837

adj.—talkative; with a smooth flow of words
The talk-show host is a **voluble** speaker.

Questions

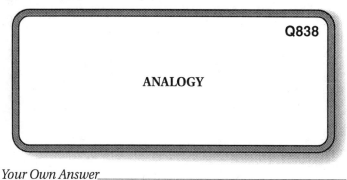

Q838

ANALOGY

*Your Own Answer*_____

_____

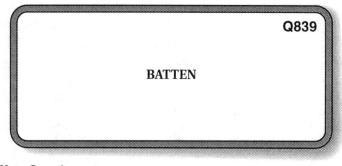

Q839

BATTEN

*Your Own Answer*_____

_____

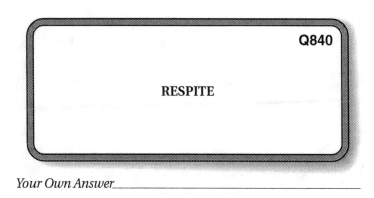

Q840

RESPITE

*Your Own Answer*_____

_____

Correct Answers

n.—similarity; correlation; parallelism

The teacher used an **analogy** to describe the two leaders.

1.v.; 2. n—1. to thrive by feeding, grow fat; 2. small board of wood used to secure, reinforce or cover

1. The turkey was **battened** with food before Thanksgiving to ensure that he would be plump for the holiday.
2. The crew was ordered to **batten** down the hatches of the ship.

n.—a reprieve

The team was given a **respite** from the long practice schedule.

Questions

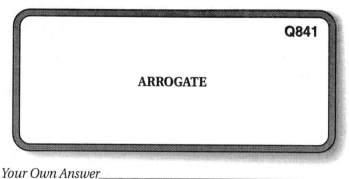

Q841

ARROGATE

*Your Own Answer*_____

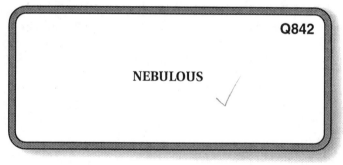

Q842

NEBULOUS

*Your Own Answer*_____

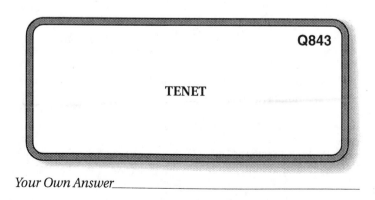

Q843

TENET

*Your Own Answer*_____

Correct Answers

A841

v.—to assume presumptuously

The teenager **arrogated** that he should be able to use his father's car whenever he desired.

A842

adj.—unclear or vague

The couple became lost on their way because they had **nebulous** directions.

A843

n.—a principle accepted as authoritative

The **tenets** of socialism were explained in the book.

Questions

Q844

ARID

*Your Own Answer*_____

Q845

FANATIC

*Your Own Answer*_____

Q846

TERSE

*Your Own Answer*_____

Correct Answers

A844

adj.—extremely dry; parched; barren; unimaginative

The terrain is so **arid** that only the very hardiest species can survive.

A845

n.—enthusiast; extremist

The terrorist group was comprised of **fanatics** who wanted to destroy those who disagreed with them.

A846

adj.—concise

The **terse** speech contained only the essential comments.

Questions

DESULTORY

*Your Own Answer*_____

EXCULPATE

*Your Own Answer*_____

TIMBRE

*Your Own Answer*_____

Correct Answers

A847

adj.—moving in a random, directionless manner

The thefts were occurring in a **desultory** manner, making them difficult to track.

A848

v.—to free from guilt

The therapy session will **exculpate** the man from his guilty feelings.

A849

n.—the quality of sound which distinguishes one from another

The **timbre** of guitar music is different from that of piano music.

Questions

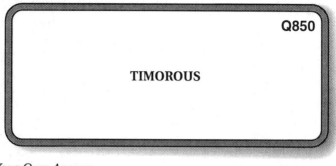

Q850

TIMOROUS

*Your Own Answer*_____

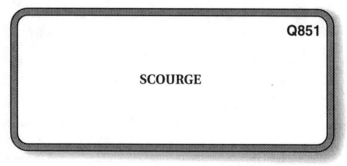

Q851

SCOURGE

*Your Own Answer*_____

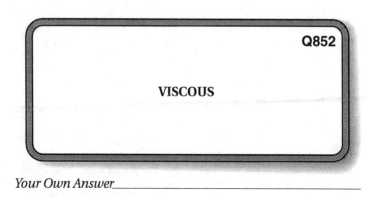

Q852

VISCOUS

*Your Own Answer*_____

Correct Answers

A850

adj.—lacking courage; timid
The **timorous** child hid behind his parents.

A851

v.—to whip severely
The trainer will **scourge** the animal if it attacks someone.

A852

adj.—thick and sticky (said of fluids)
The tree emitted a **viscous** material.

Questions

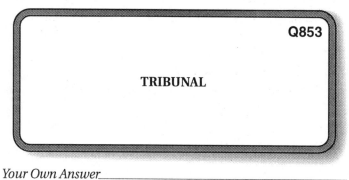

Q853

TRIBUNAL

*Your Own Answer*_____

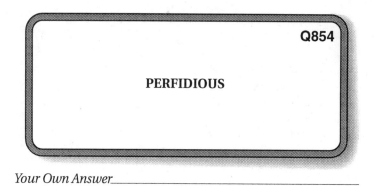

Q854

PERFIDIOUS

*Your Own Answer*_____

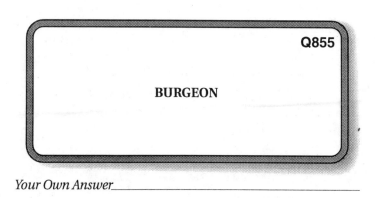

Q855

BURGEON

*Your Own Answer*_____

Correct Answers

A853

n.—the seat of judgment

The **tribunal** heard the case of the burglary.

A854

adj.—faithless; treacherous

The trust between the business associates was broken after the **perfidious** actions of one of the partners.

A855

v.—to grow or develop quickly

The tumor appeared to **burgeon** more quickly than normal.

Questions

Q856

TURBID

*Your Own Answer*_____

Q857

TURPITUDE

*Your Own Answer*_____

Q858

PINIONED

*Your Own Answer*_____

Correct Answers

A856

adj.—thick and dense; cloudy

The **turbid** green waters of the lake prevented them from seeing the bottom.

A857

n.—vileness

The **turpitude** of the action caused a rage among the people.

A858

adj.—bound

The two rafts were **pinioned** by steel wire.

Questions

Q859

CONVERGE

*Your Own Answer*_____

Q860

HEFTY

*Your Own Answer*_____

Q861

INDOMITABLE

*Your Own Answer*_____

Correct Answers

A859

v.—to move toward one point (opposite: diverge)
The two roads **converge** at the corner.

A860

adj.—heavy or powerful
The unabridged dictionary makes for a **hefty** book.

A861

adj.—not easily discouraged or defeated
The underdog candidate had an **indomitable** spirit.

Questions

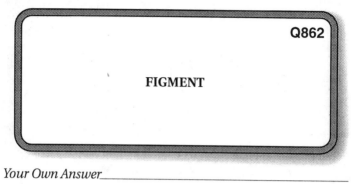

Q862

FIGMENT

*Your Own Answer*_____

_____

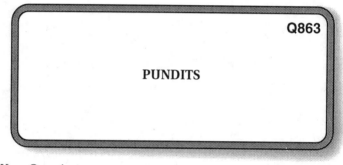

Q863

PUNDITS

*Your Own Answer*_____

_____

Q864

UNWONTED

*Your Own Answer*_____

_____

Correct Answers

A862

n.—something made up in the mind
The unicorn on the hill was a **figment** of his imagination.

A863

n.—a person claiming to have great knowledge
The university is full of **pundits**.

A864

adj.—rare
The **unwonted** raise would be the only one received for a few years.

Questions

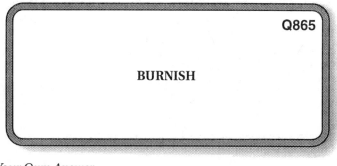

Q865

BURNISH

*Your Own Answer*_____

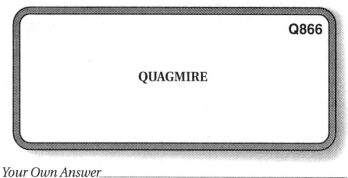

Q866

QUAGMIRE

*Your Own Answer*_____

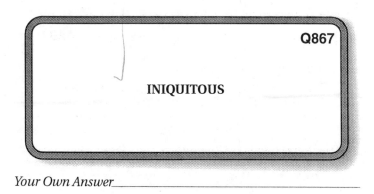

Q867

INIQUITOUS

*Your Own Answer*_____

Correct Answers

A865

v.—to polish by rubbing

The vase needed to be **burnished** to restore its beauty.

A866

n.—marshy land

The vehicle became stuck in the **quagmire**.

A867

adj.—wicked; unjust

The verbal abuse towards the man was truly **iniquitous**.

Questions

CABAL

*Your Own Answer*_____

VISCID

*Your Own Answer*_____

PALLID

*Your Own Answer*_____

Correct Answers

A868

n.—a group of persons joined by a secret
The very idea that there could be a **cabal** cast suspicion on the whole operation.

A869

adj.—thick; syrupy; sticky
The **viscid** mixture seemed to be honey.

A870

adj.—pale in color
The visitor left the hospital room with a **pallid** face.

Questions

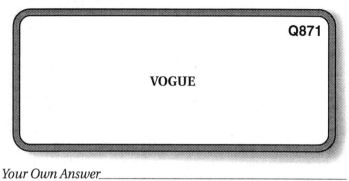

Q871

VOGUE

*Your Own Answer*_____

_____

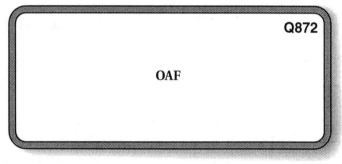

Q872

OAF

*Your Own Answer*_____

_____

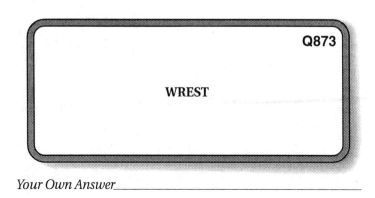

Q873

WREST

*Your Own Answer*_____

_____

Correct Answers

A871

n.—that which is accepted for the time, esp. in fashion

The **vogue** was high-heeled shoes and long skirts.

A872

n.—a clumsy, dumb person

The waiter has been called an **oaf** ever since he dropped the tray.

A873

v.—to usurp forcefully; to take from

The warriors **wrested** the power from the king.

Questions

REGAL

*Your Own Answer*_____

WELTER

*Your Own Answer*_____

DIVERGE

*Your Own Answer*_____

Correct Answers

A874

adj.—stately
The well-bred woman behaves in a **regal** manner.

A875

n.—a confused mass; turmoil
The **welter** moved from street to street to escape
the fire.

A876

v.—to separate; to split
The wide, long river **diverged** into two distinct
rivers, never again to join.

Questions

Q877

WILY

*Your Own Answer*_____

Q878

CORROBORATE

*Your Own Answer*_____

Q879

AVER

*Your Own Answer*_____

Correct Answers

A877

adj.—sly

The **wily** explanation was meant to confuse the investigator.

A878

v.—to confirm the validity

The witness must **corroborate** the prisoner's story if she is to be set free.

A879

v.—to affirm

The witness was able to **aver** the identity of the defendant.

Questions

Q880

WIZENED

*Your Own Answer*_____

_____

Q881

BAUBLE

*Your Own Answer*_____

_____

Q882

ERUDITE

*Your Own Answer*_____

_____

Correct Answers

A880

adj.—shriveled; withered
The **wizened** face of the old man was covered by his hat.

A881

n.—a showy yet useless thing
The woman had many **baubles** on her bookshelf.

A882

adj.—having a wide knowledge acquired through reading
The woman was so **erudite** she could discuss any subject.

Questions

Q883

POMMEL

*Your Own Answer*_____

Q884

ABNEGATION

*Your Own Answer*_____

Q885

THRALL

*Your Own Answer*_____

Correct Answers

A883

n.—the rounded, upward-projecting front of a saddle

The woman was so nervous about being on the horse she would not let go of the **pommel**.

A884

v.—to deny oneself

The priest **abnegated** a secular life upon receiving his ordination.

A885

n.—a slave

The worker was treated like a **thrall**, having to work many hours of overtime.

Questions

IMPASSE

*Your Own Answer*_____

VILIFY

*Your Own Answer*_____

IMBUE

*Your Own Answer*_____

Correct Answers

A886

n.—a situation that has no solution or escape

The workers and the administration were at an **impasse** in their negotiations.

A887

v.—to speak abusively of

The workers too often **vilify** an employer when upset with working conditions.

A888

v.—to soak or stain

The wound will **imbue** the shirt in blood.

Questions

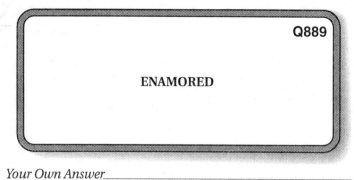

Q889

ENAMORED

*Your Own Answer*_____

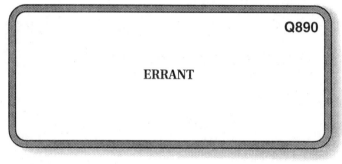

Q890

ERRANT

*Your Own Answer*_____

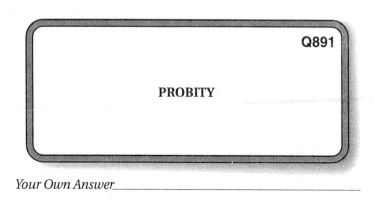

Q891

PROBITY

*Your Own Answer*_____

Correct Answers

A889

adj.—filled with love and desire
The young couple is **enamored** with each other.

A890

adj.—roving in search of adventure
The young man set out across country on an **errant** expedition.

A891

n.—honesty
The young man's **probity** was reassuring to the fearful parent.

Questions

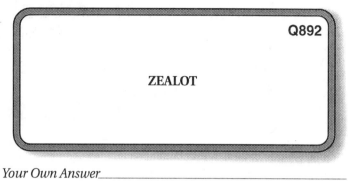

Q892

ZEALOT

*Your Own Answer*_____

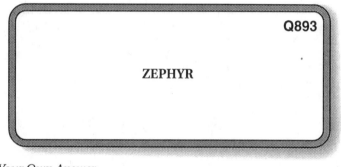

Q893

ZEPHYR

*Your Own Answer*_____

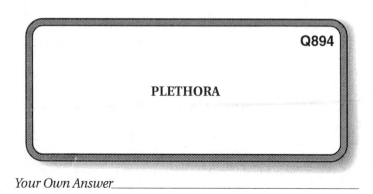

Q894

PLETHORA

*Your Own Answer*_____

Correct Answers

A892

n.—a fanatical person
The **zealot** refused to leave until he saw the preacher.

A893

n.—a west wind; a gentle breeze
The **zephyr** blew the boat slowly across the lake.

A894

n.—a superabundance
There was a **plethora** of food at the feast.

Questions

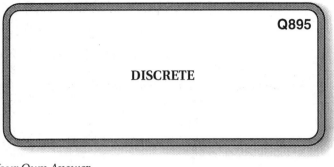

Q895

DISCRETE

*Your Own Answer*_____

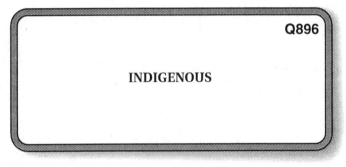

Q896

INDIGENOUS

*Your Own Answer*_____

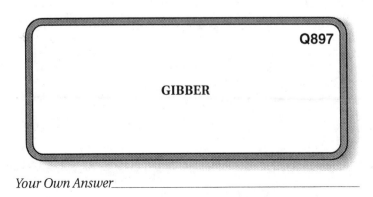

Q897

GIBBER

*Your Own Answer*_____

Correct Answers

A895

adj.—separate; composed of distinct parts
There were four **discrete** aspects to the architecture of the home.

A896

adj.—native to a region; inborn or innate
These plants are **indigenous** to all of the western states.

A897

v.—to rapidly speak unintelligibly
They did not want him to represent their position in front of the committee since he was likely to **gibber.**

Questions

ETHNIC

*Your Own Answer*_____

_____

FERVENT

*Your Own Answer*_____

_____

APATHY

*Your Own Answer*_____

_____

Correct Answers

A898

adj.—designating or of any of the basic groups/divisions of humankind, or of a heterogeneous population as distinguished by customs, culture, common language, etc.

They enjoyed going to the town for lunch because of its **ethnic** restaurants.

A899

adj.—passionate; intense

They have a **fervent** relationship that keeps them together every minute of every day.

A900

n.—lack of emotion or interest

They may have the right to vote, but **apathy** is apparent when few people actually turn out to vote.

Questions

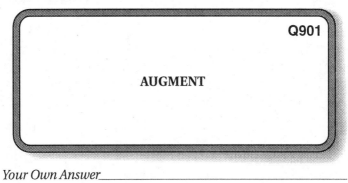

Q901

AUGMENT

*Your Own Answer*_____

Q902

INELUCTABLE

*Your Own Answer*_____

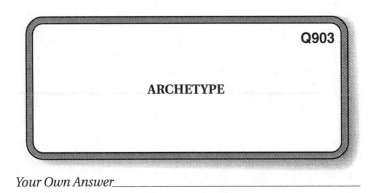

Q903

ARCHETYPE

*Your Own Answer*_____

Correct Answers

A901

v.—to make greater

They were able to **augment** their savings over a period of time.

A902

adj.—inevitable

They were prepared for the **ineluctable** disaster.

A903

n.—an original pattern or model; a prototype

This man was the **archetype** for scores of fictional characters.

Questions

Q904

QUINTESSENCE

*Your Own Answer*_____

Q905

DILETTANTE

*Your Own Answer*_____

Q906

ENIGMA

*Your Own Answer*_____

Correct Answers

A904

n.—the pure essence of anything

This story is the **quintessence** of American fiction.

A905

n.—a person taking up an art or activity merely for amusement

Despite the money he put into painting lessons, the man was more of a **dilettante** than a serious painter.

A906

n.—a mystery; a secret; a perplexity

To all of the searchers, the missing child's location remained a great **enigma**.

Questions

Q907

GERRYMANDER

*Your Own Answer*_____

Q908

ACRIMONY

*Your Own Answer*_____

Q909

CHAGRIN

*Your Own Answer*_____

Correct Answers

A907

v.—to gain advantage by manipulating unfairly

To **gerrymander** during negotiations is considered unfair.

A908

n.—sharpness or bitterness in language or manner

To hear such **acrimony** from the normally soft-spoken board member unnerved her colleagues.

A909

n.—a feeling of embarrassment due to failure or disappointment

To the **chagrin** of the inventor, the machine did not work.

Questions

Q910

TRUCULENT

*Your Own Answer*_____

_____

Q911

SALUTATORY

*Your Own Answer*_____

_____

Q912

GAUCHE

*Your Own Answer*_____

_____

Correct Answers

A910

adj.—fierce; savage; cruel
Truculent fighting broke out in the war-torn country.

A911

adj.—of or containing greetings
Two messengers were sent to the new neighbors with a **salutatory** letter.

A912

adj.—awkward; lacking social grace
Unfortunately, the girl was too **gauche** to fit into high society.

Questions

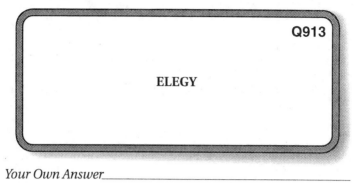

Q913

ELEGY

*Your Own Answer*_____

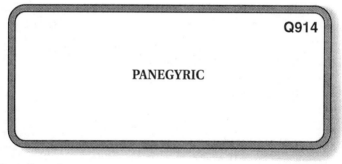

Q914

PANEGYRIC

*Your Own Answer*_____

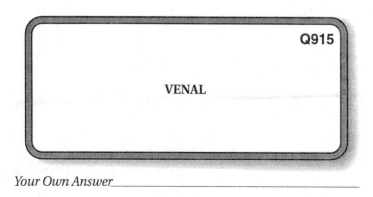

Q915

VENAL

*Your Own Answer*_____

Correct Answers

A913

n.—a poem of lament and praise for the dead

Upon conclusion of the **elegy**, the casket was closed.

A914

n.—a formal speech or writing praising a person or event

Upon his retirement, he received a **panegyric** from many of his associates.

A915

adj.—able to be purchased, as by a bribe

Venal employees caused the downfall of the company.

Questions

Q916

VOCIFEROUS

*Your Own Answer*_____

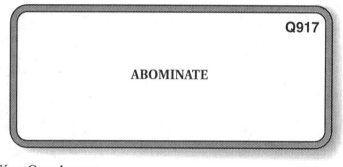

Q917

ABOMINATE

*Your Own Answer*_____

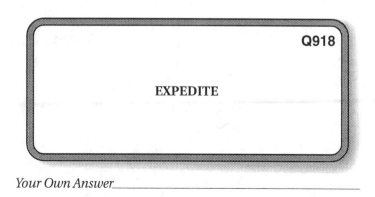

Q918

EXPEDITE

*Your Own Answer*_____

Correct Answers

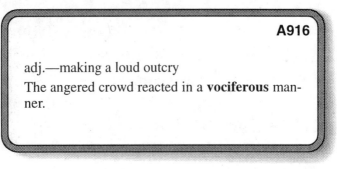

A916

adj.—making a loud outcry
The angered crowd reacted in a **vociferous** manner.

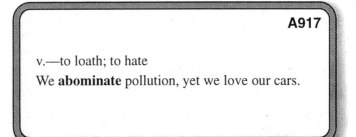

A917

v.—to loath; to hate
We **abominate** pollution, yet we love our cars.

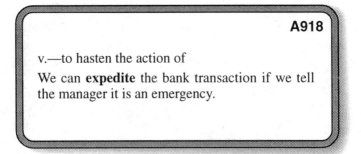

A918

v.—to hasten the action of
We can **expedite** the bank transaction if we tell the manager it is an emergency.

Questions

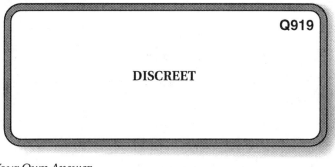

Q919

DISCREET

*Your Own Answer*_____

_____

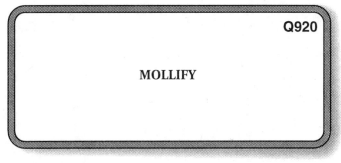

Q920

MOLLIFY

*Your Own Answer*_____

_____

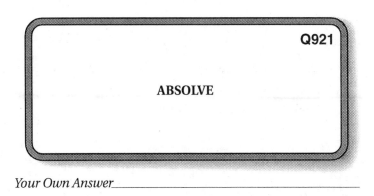

Q921

ABSOLVE

*Your Own Answer*_____

_____

Correct Answers

A919

adj.—showing good judgment in conduct; prudent

We confided our secret in Mary because we knew she'd be **discreet**.

A920

v.—to soften; to make less intense

We used our hands to **mollify** the sound of our giggling.

A921

v.—to forgive; to acquit

The man was **absolved** of his rude act after he said he was sorry.

Questions

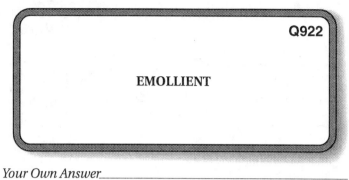

Q922

EMOLLIENT

*Your Own Answer*_____

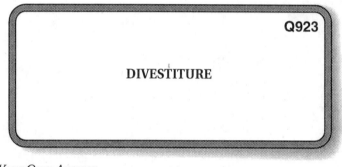

Q923

DIVESTITURE

*Your Own Answer*_____

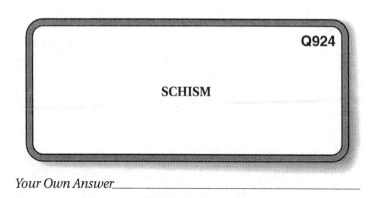

Q924

SCHISM

*Your Own Answer*_____

Correct Answers

A922

adj.—softening or soothing to the skin

When hands become dry, it may be necessary to soothe them with an **emollient** lotion.

A923

n.—the act of stripping

The tree could not survive the **divestiture** of the wind, so it lost all of its leaves.

A924

n.—a division in an organized group

When the group could not decide on a plan of action, a **schism** occurred.

Questions

Q925

DECIDUOUS

*Your Own Answer*_____

Q926

IGNEOUS

*Your Own Answer*_____

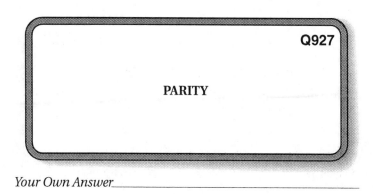

Q927

PARITY

*Your Own Answer*_____

Correct Answers

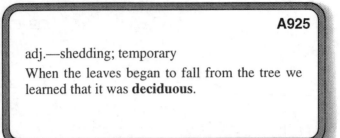

A925

adj.—shedding; temporary

When the leaves began to fall from the tree we learned that it was **deciduous**.

A926

adj.—having the nature of fire; formed by volcanic action

When the sun shone upon it, the material took on an **igneous** quality.

A927

n.—the state of being the same in power, value, or rank

When the younger brother was promoted to co-president with the elder son, it established **parity** between the two.

Questions

SANGUINE

*Your Own Answer*_____

STOLID

*Your Own Answer*_____

DOTING

*Your Own Answer*_____

Correct Answers

A928

adj.—hopeful; confident
With a **sanguine** nod, the interviewee entered the office.

A929

adj.—showing little emotion
With a **stolid** expression, the man walked away from the confrontation.

A930

adj.—excessively fond of
With great joy, the **doting** father held the toddler.

Questions

Q931

SUBTLETY

*Your Own Answer*_____

Q932

TREPIDATION

*Your Own Answer*_____

Q933

INTRANSIGENT

*Your Own Answer*_____

Correct Answers

A931

n.—the state of being fine or delicate in perception or meaning

The painting of the crowded beach captured the feeling of summertime with great **subtlety**.

A932

n.—fearful uncertainty

With great **trepidation**, the boy entered the water for the first time.

A933

adj.—uncompromising

No amount of arguing could change her **intransigent** position.

Questions

Q934

GAINSAY

*Your Own Answer*_____

_____

Q935

STOIC

*Your Own Answer*_____

_____

Q936

ACCRETION

*Your Own Answer*_____

_____

Correct Answers

A934

v.—to speak against; to contradict; to deny

With Senator Bowker the only one to **gainsay** it, the bill passed overwhelmingly.

A935

adj.—not easily excited

With **stoic** obedience, the child sat quietly on the chair.

A936

n.—growth by addition

With the **accretion** of new members, the club doubled its original size.

Questions

Q937

COVENANT

*Your Own Answer*_____

_____

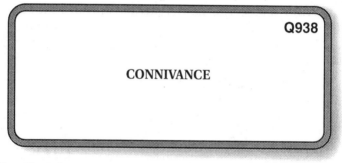

Q938

CONNIVANCE

*Your Own Answer*_____

_____

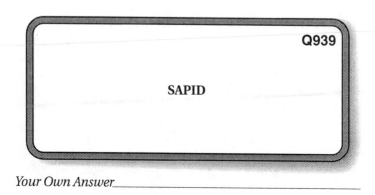

Q939

SAPID

*Your Own Answer*_____

_____

Correct Answers

A937

n.—a binding and solemn agreement
With the exchange of vows, the **covenant** was complete.

A938

n.—a secret cooperation in wrongdoing
With the guard's **connivance**, the convict was able to make his escape.

A939

adj.—having a pleasant taste
Yellow and blue icing covered the **sapid** pastry.

BLANK CARDS
To Make Up
Your Own Questions

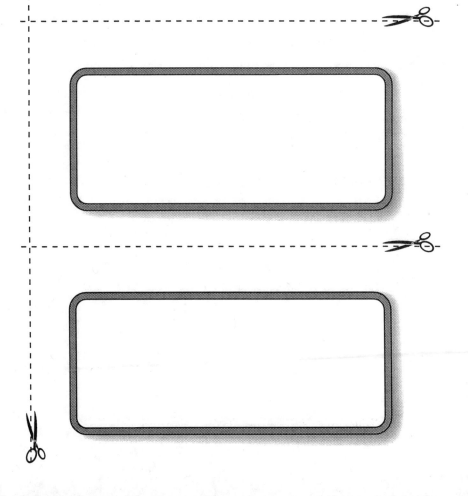

CORRECT ANSWERS

for

Your Own Questions

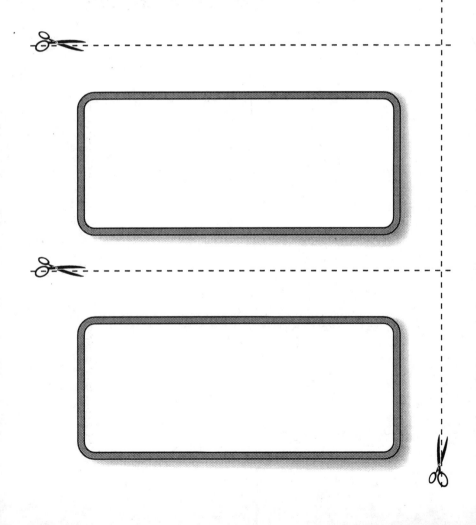

Blank Cards for
Your Own Questions

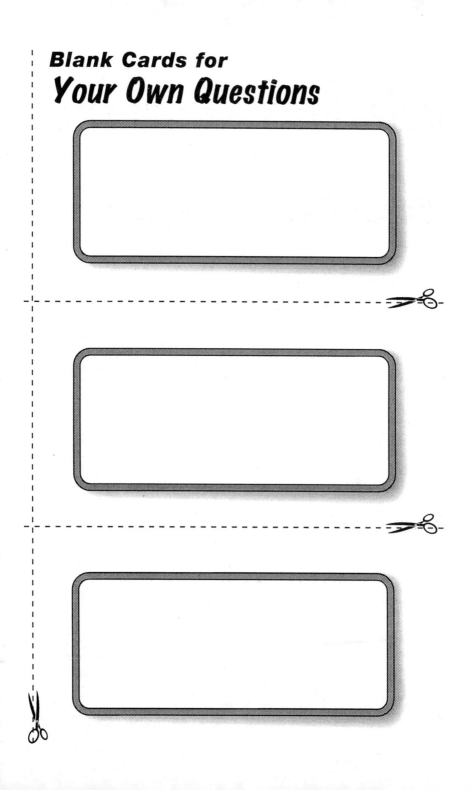

Correct Answers

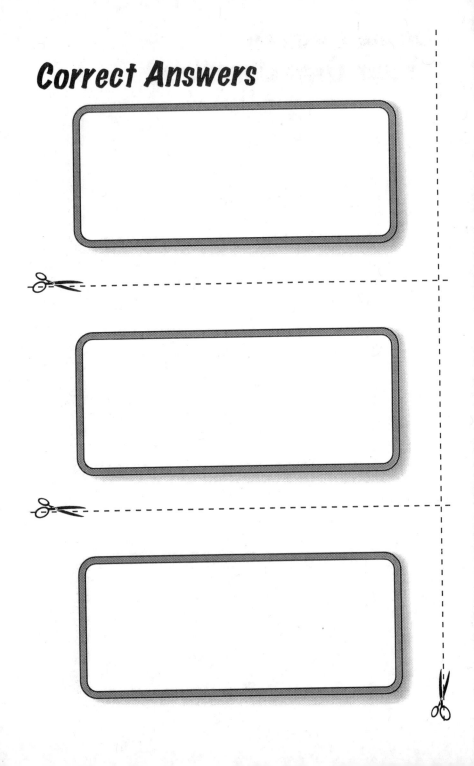

Blank Cards for
Your Own Questions

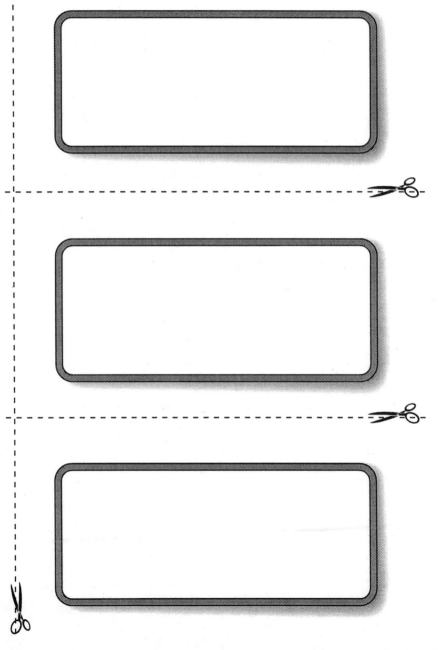

Correct Answers

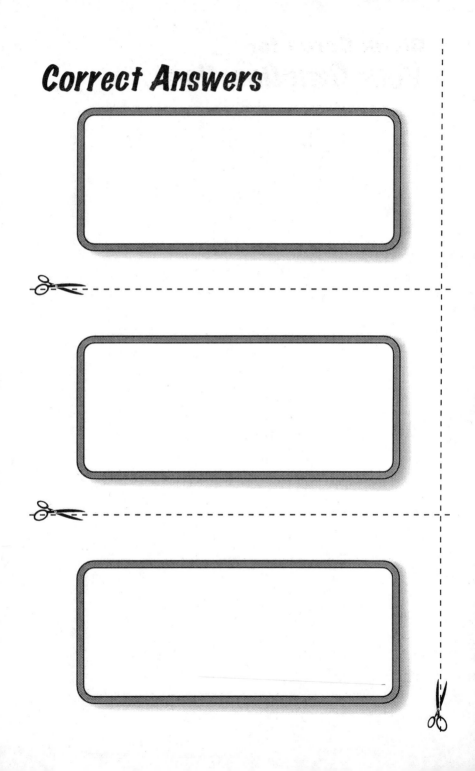

Blank Cards for
Your Own Questions

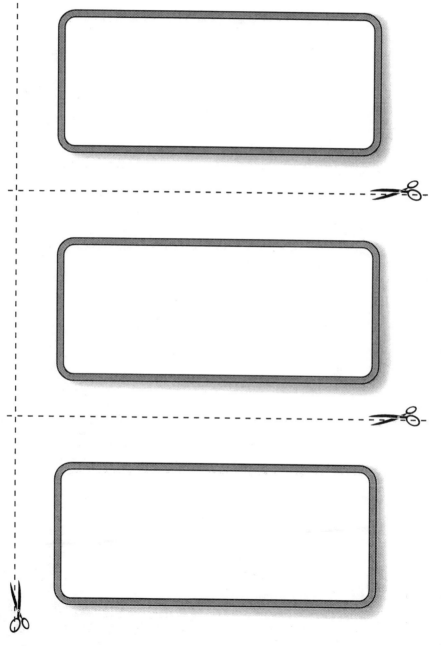

Correct Answers

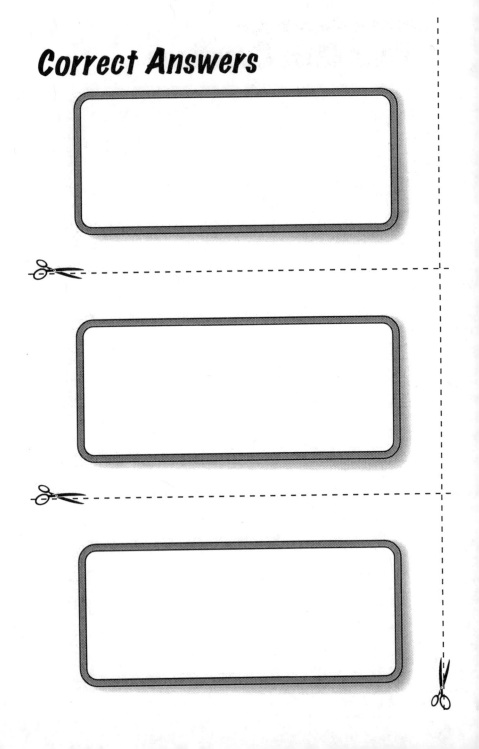

Blank Cards for
Your Own Questions

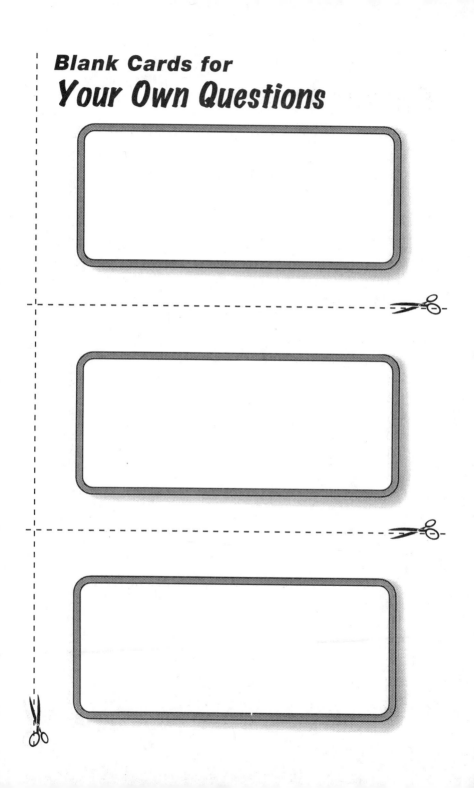

Correct Answers

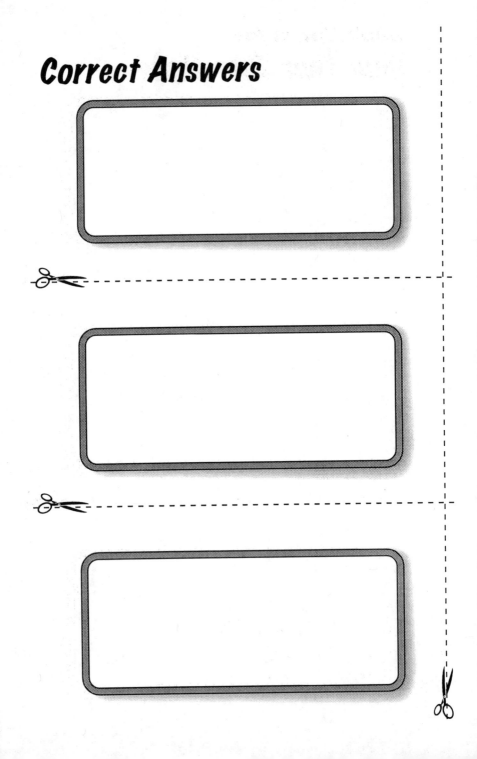

Blank Cards for
Your Own Questions

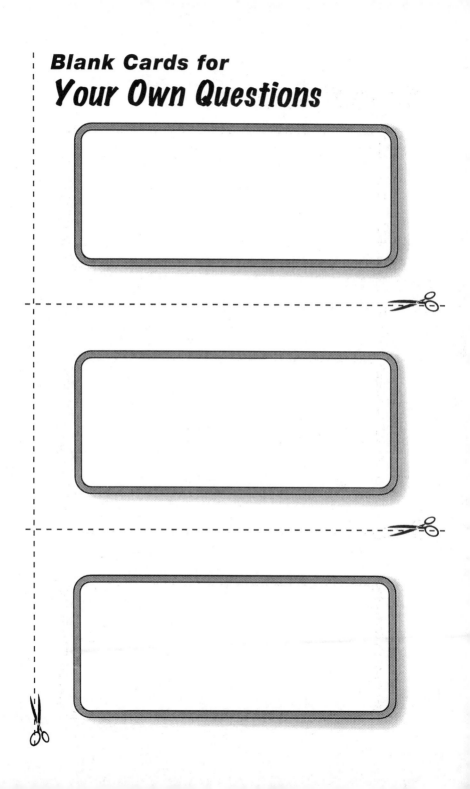

Correct Answers

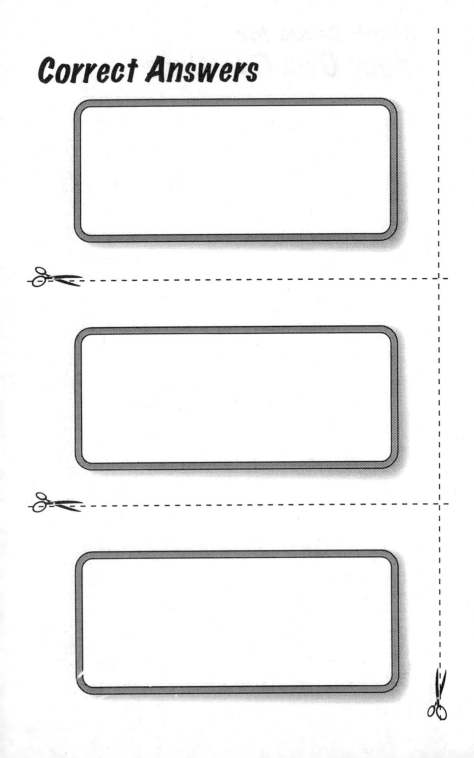

Blank Cards for
Your Own Questions

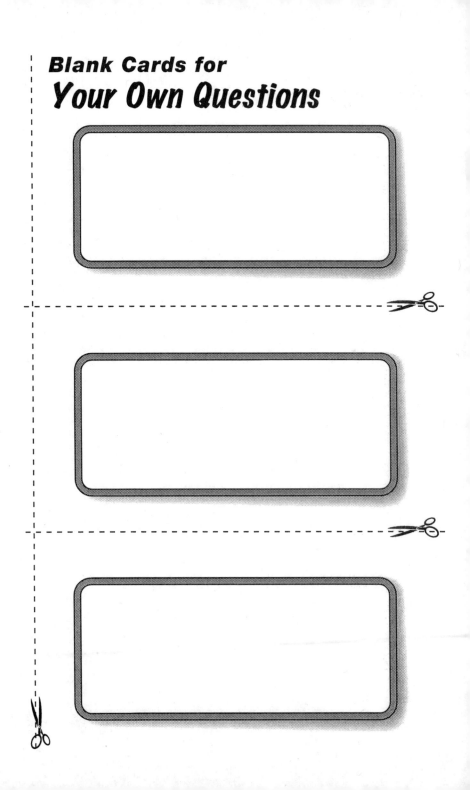

Correct Answers

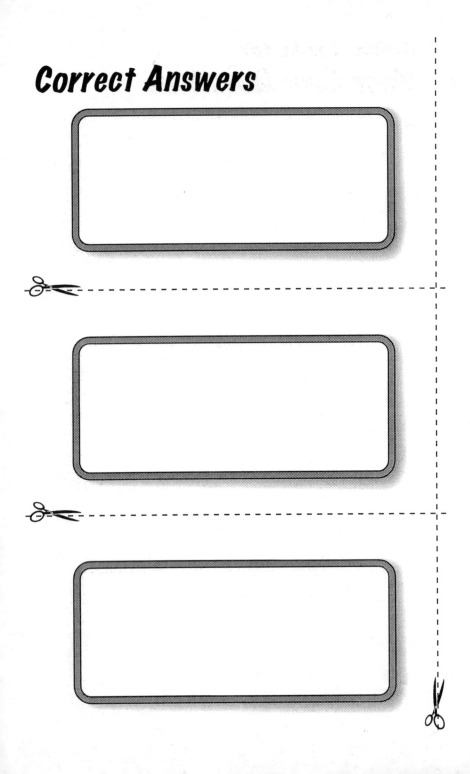

Blank Cards for
Your Own Questions

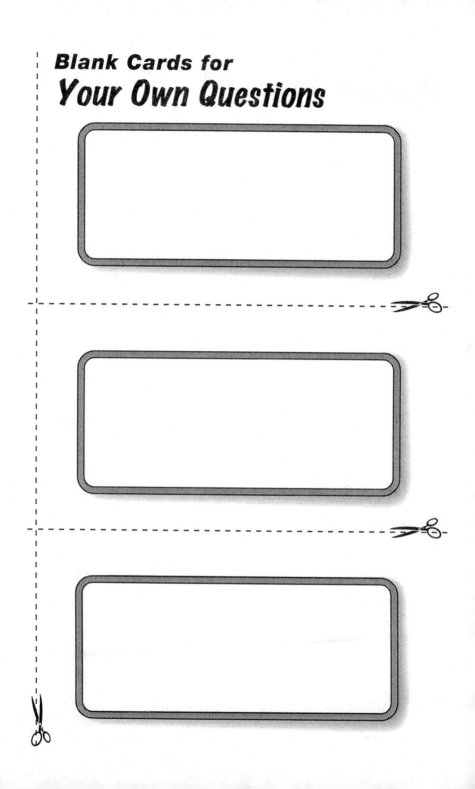

Correct Answers

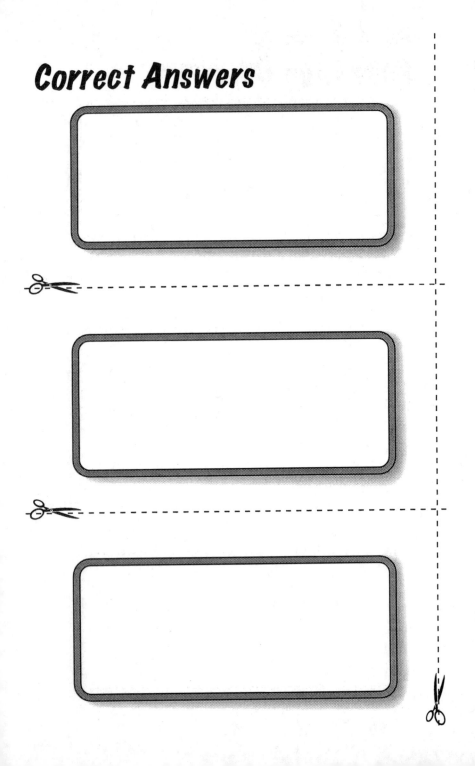

Blank Cards for
Your Own Questions

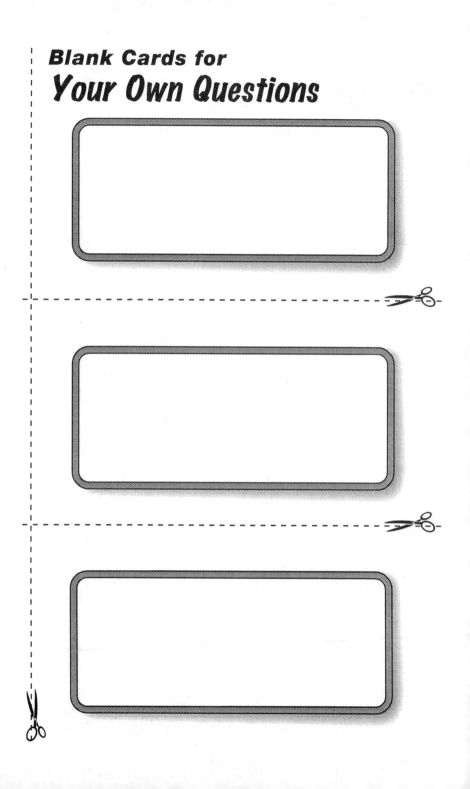

Correct Answers

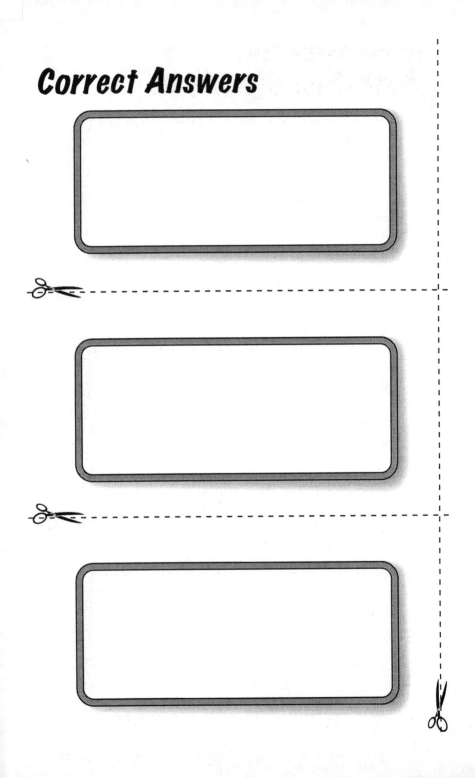

Blank Cards for
Your Own Questions

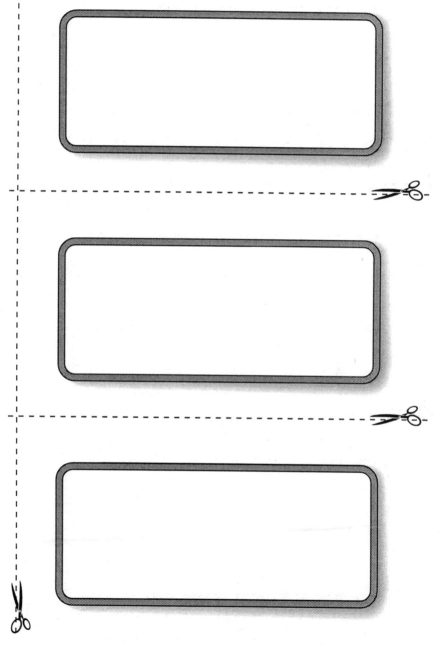

Correct Answers

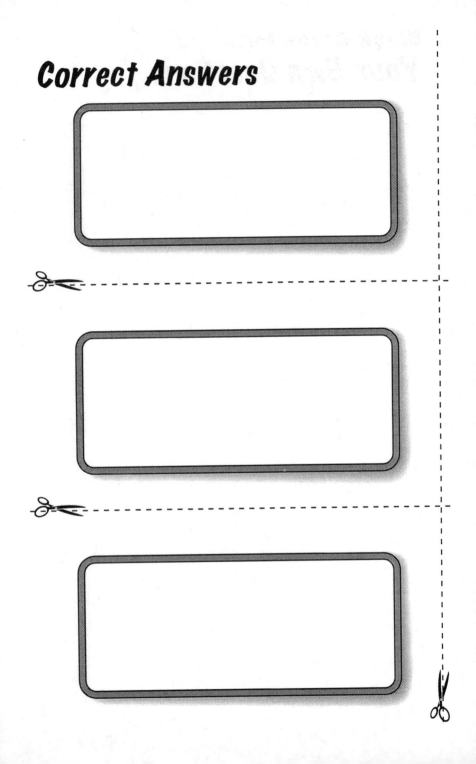

Blank Cards for
Your Own Questions

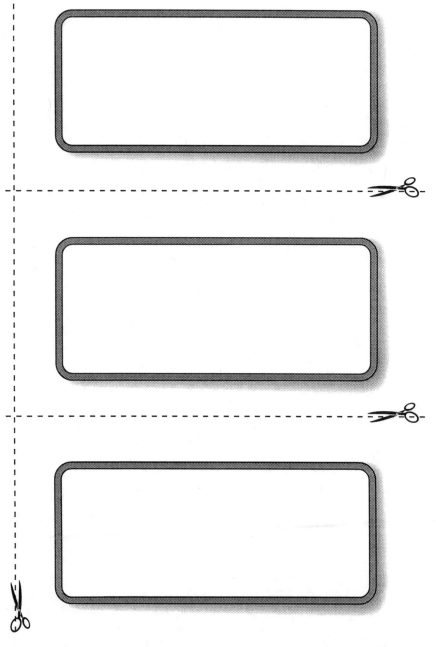

Correct Answers

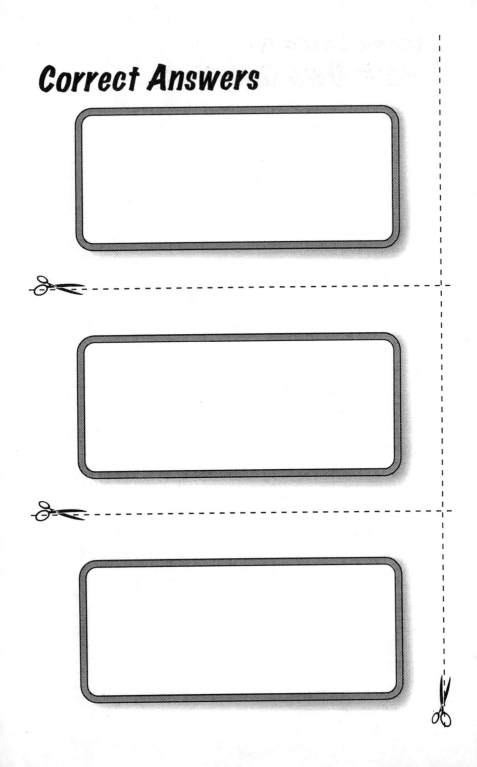

Blank Cards for
Your Own Questions

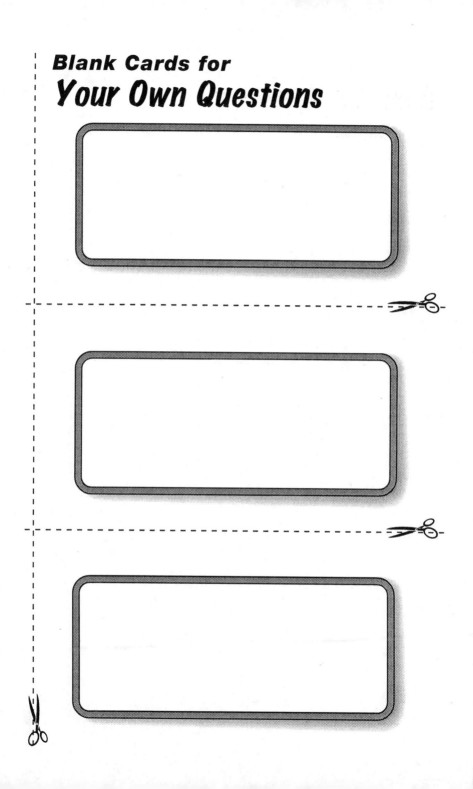

Correct Answers

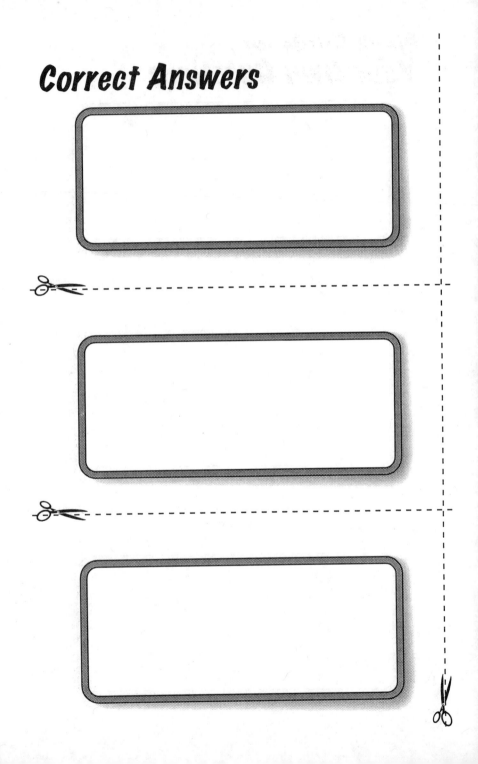

Blank Cards for
Your Own Questions

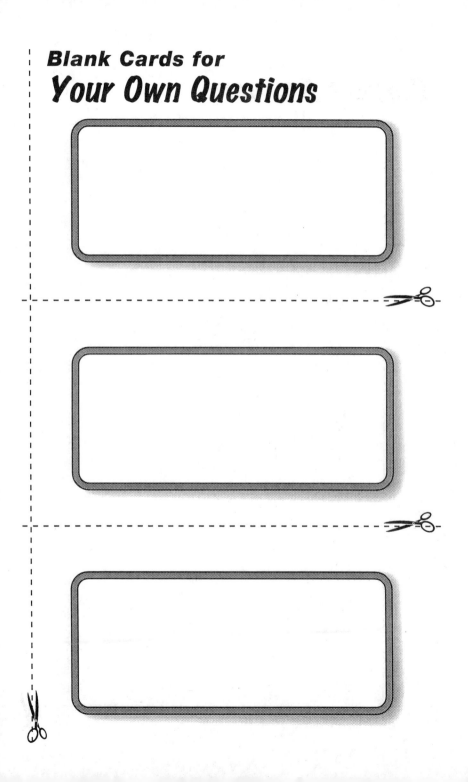

Correct Answers

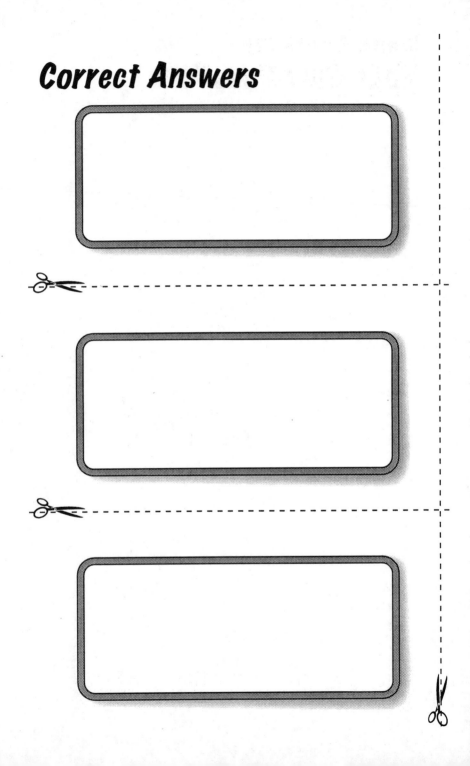

Blank Cards for
Your Own Questions

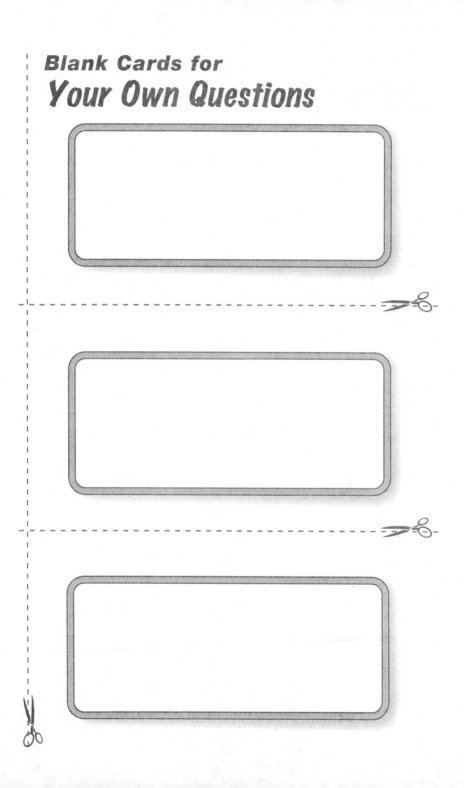

Correct Answers

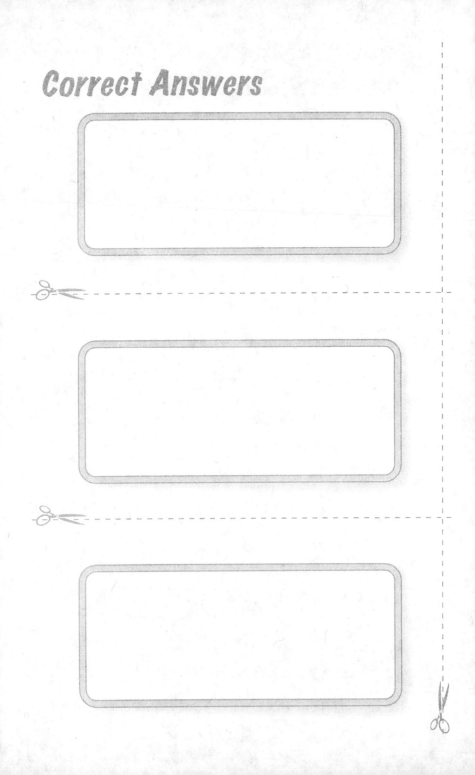

Blank Cards for
Your Own Questions

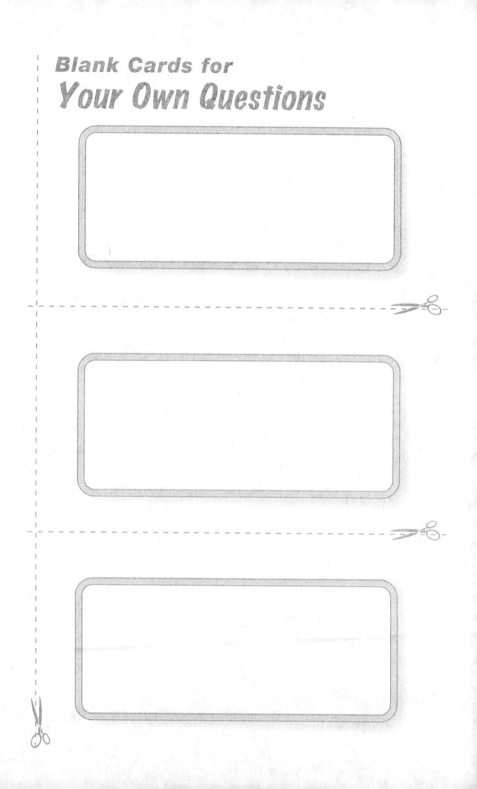

Correct Answers

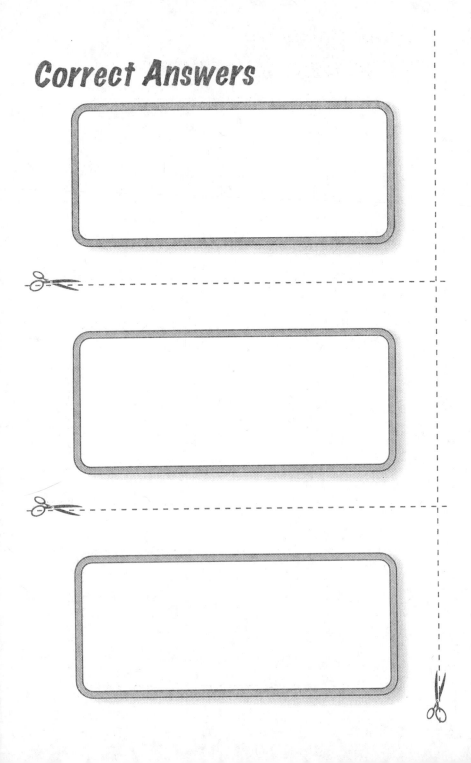

Blank Cards for
Your Own Questions

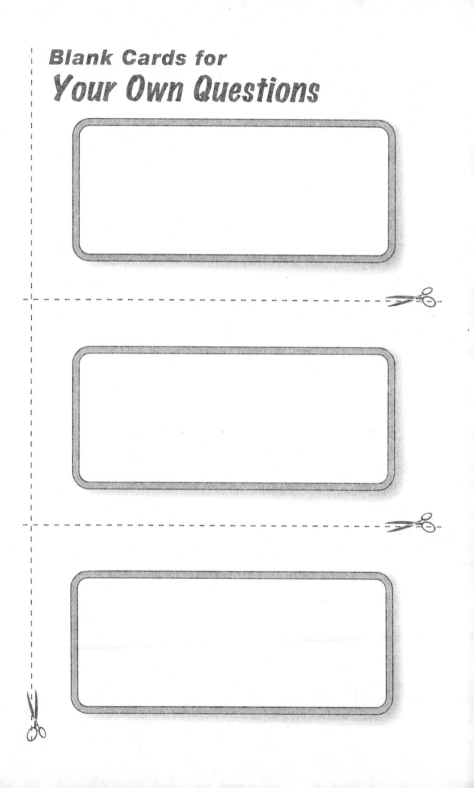

Correct Answers

Blank Cards for
Your Own Questions

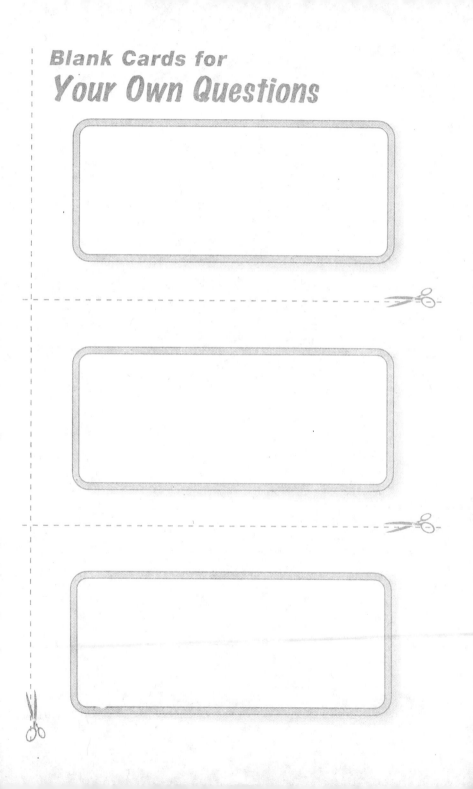

Correct Answers

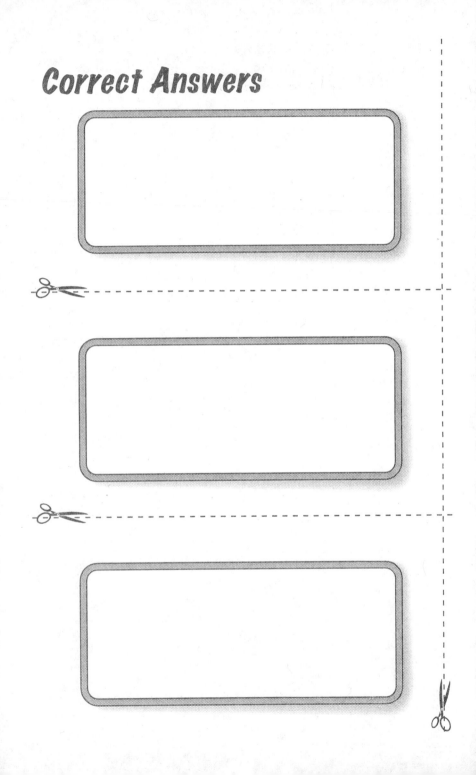

Blank Cards for
Your Own Questions

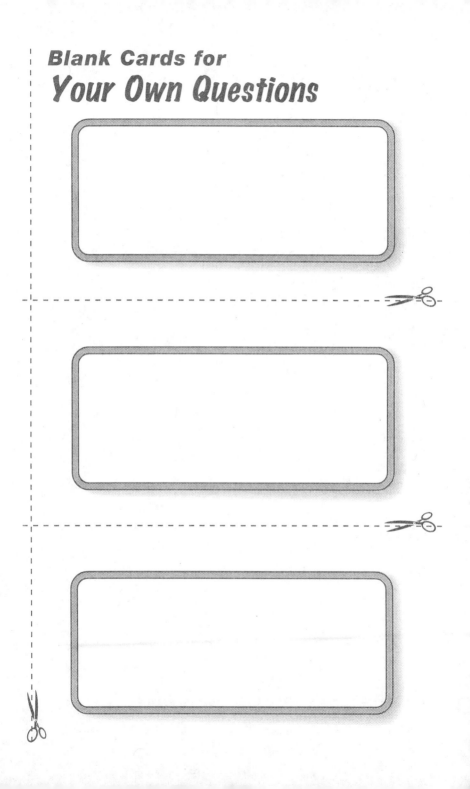

Correct Answers

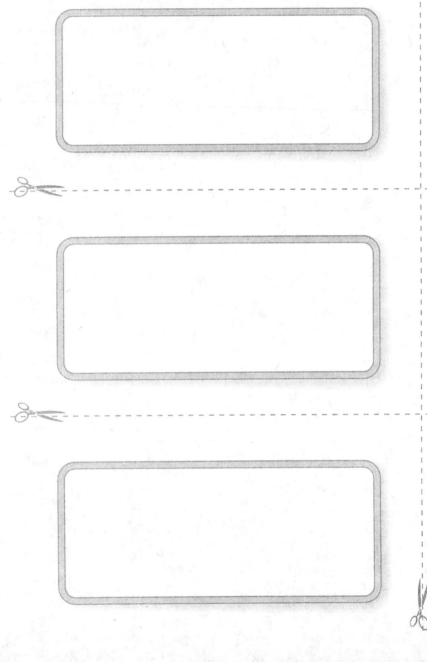

Blank Cards for
Your Own Questions

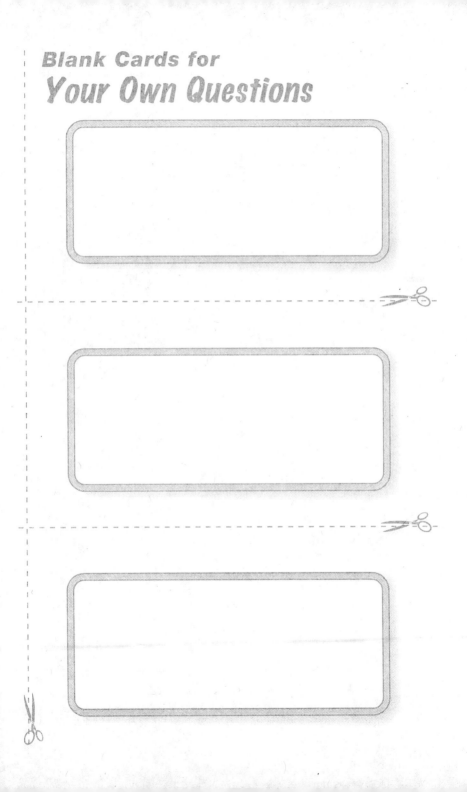

Correct Answers

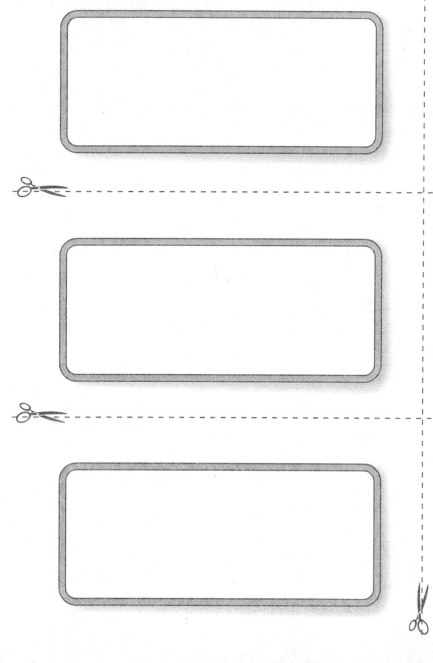

Blank Cards for
Your Own Questions

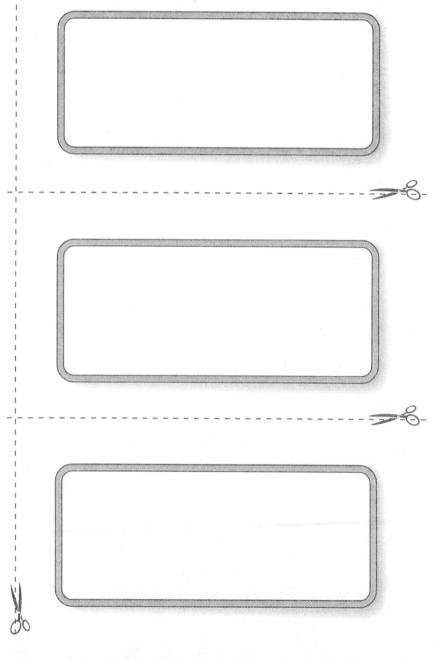

Correct Answers

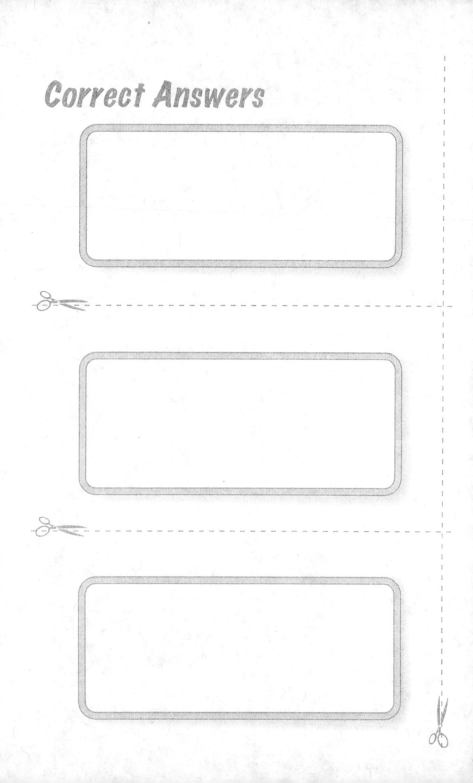

Blank Cards for
Your Own Questions

Correct Answers

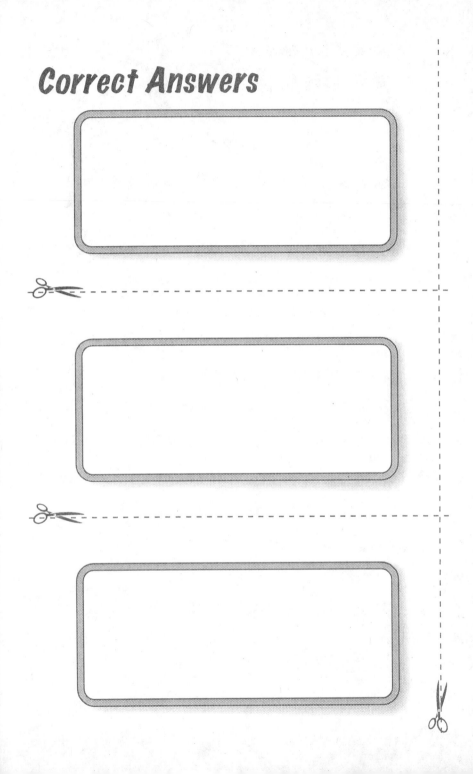

Blank Cards for
Your Own Questions

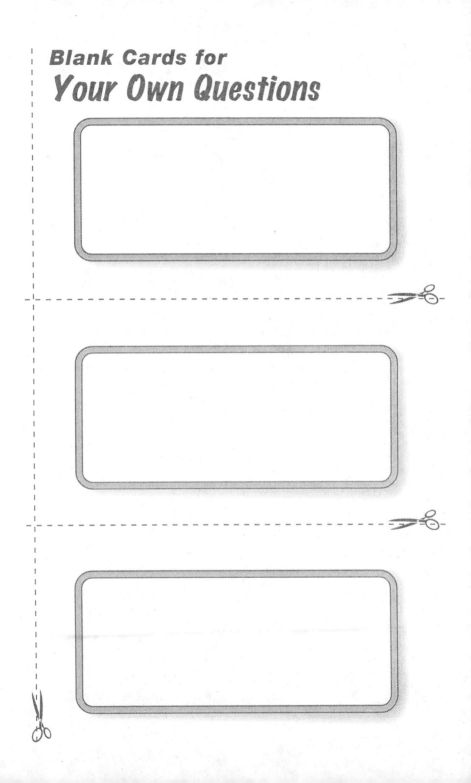

Correct Answers

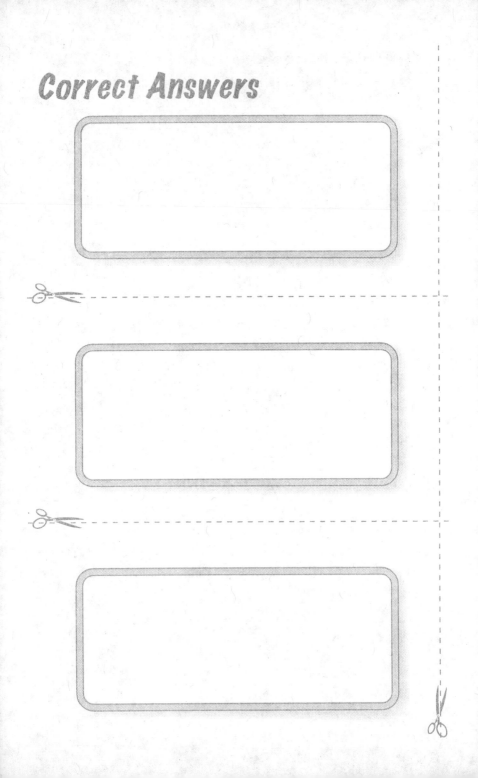

Blank Cards for
Your Own Questions

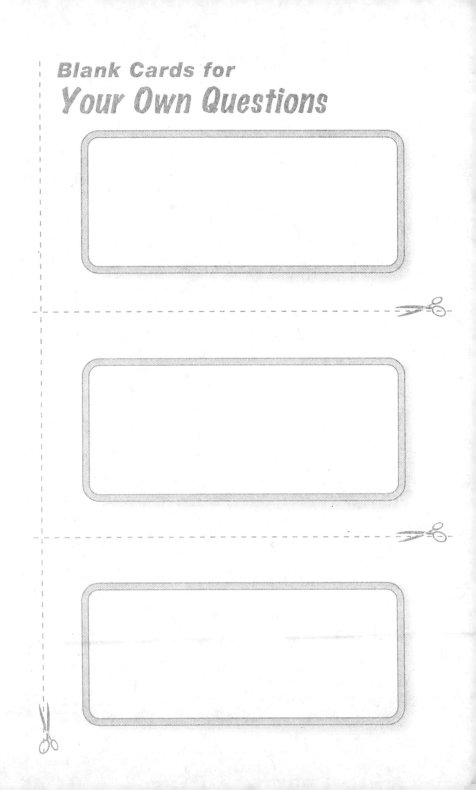

Correct Answers

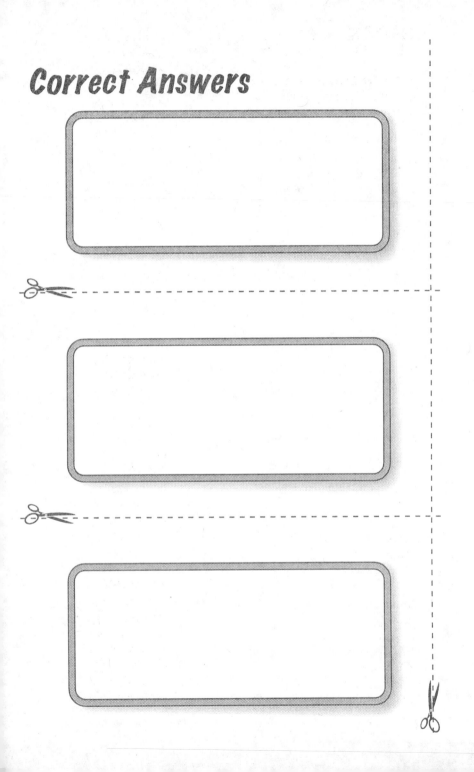

INDEX

augment, 901
auspicious, 44
austere, 99
autocracy, 470
autocrat, 471
avarice, 694
aver, 879
baleful, 824
banal, 228
baroque, 477
batten, 839
bauble, 881
beget, 660
beholden, 512
behoove, 361
bellicose, 478
beneficent, 161
benevolent, 479
bereft, 90
beseech, 808
besmirch, 811
bestial, 480
betroth, 683
biennial, 501
bilateral, 490
blasphemous, 324
blighted, 481
blithe, 482
bode, 820
bombast, 771
boor, 485
brindled, 359
broach, 239
brusque, 325
bucolic, 492
bumptious, 298
burgeon, 855
burlesque, 40
burnish, 865
cabal, 868
cache, 495
cacophony, 459

cajole, 795
caliber, 496
callow, 216
calumny, 341
canard, 497
cant, 783
caprice, 500
captious, 162
carte blanche, 553
cascade, 26
castigate, 705
cataclysm, 576
catharsis, 197
caustic, 62
cavil, 511
censure, 38
cessation, 503
chafe, 32
chaffing, 659
chagrin, 909
charlatan, 505
chary, 18
chaste, 233
chicanery, 833
choleric, 513
churlishness, 515
circumlocution, 698
circumspect, 163
clandestine, 517
cloture, 203
cloying, 212
coalesce, 491
coda, 242
codify, 665
cogent, 666
cogitate, 369
cognitive, 249
cognizant, 432
coherent, 539
cohesion, 521
cohort, 522
colloquial, 65